The BOLD AMERICAN OUTLOOK® Handbook

Handbook

A New Post-Racism Paradigm™ for the 21st Century Designed to Show Educators/Parents How to Teach America's Young People to Find Solutions to End Racism' Legacy in Their Lifetime

The Bold American Outlook

By

Anthony Maceo
Cultural Diversity Consultant

1st Books rev. 06/8/00

About the Book

The BOLD AMERICAN OUTLOOK Handbook--A New Post-Racism Paradigm™ for the 21st Century--Designed to Show Educators/Parents How to Teach America's Young People to Find Solutions to Racism's Legacy in Their Lifetime--is an unprecedented and essential handbook for educators and parents. Consisting of short, concise, thought-provoking chapters, examples and incentives, this handy guide shows educators and parents what must be taught to students/children to end racism's legacy in their lifetime. This handbook will detail how a "language of racism" in the American discourse inhibits America's ability to end racism's legacy and find solutions to our social problems. There are no simple solutions to racism's legacy, yet you'll find that *The BOLD AMERICAN OUTLOOK* is the most viable option today. This is the first in a series of books I propose to write showing Americans how they can defuse claims of racism and end racism's legacy in America's future.

Adult Americans MUST establish a "Post-Racism Paradigm"--a mode of thought beyond the concepts of "races"--for young people if we want to continue our position as a world leader and, more importantly, if we indeed want to end this nation's most enduring social cancer--racism's legacy. *The BOLD AMERICAN OUTLOOK* does not have an ethnocentric agenda. Instead, *The BOLD AMERICAN OUTLOOK* has a "let's show American young people how to improve their future human relations without the old paradigms of 'race' agenda." **You'll find that the included BOLD AMERICAN OUTLOOK Principles are a vital asset for that agenda and for all Americans.**

If we do not act quickly toward establishing a BOLD AMERICAN OUTLOOK, which will prevent young people from inheriting the false "racial" concepts that we adults unfortunately inherited, then young people will become infested with the long-festering cancer of racism. Racism's legacy is capable of consuming young people and this nation into a "race" war because of the historical momentum it has generated AND because we adults have not afforded them a "post-racism paradigm" to counter this historical momentum.

Recent events only graphically demonstrate that the greatest enemy this nation has today is us. We create and re-create our own "intra-American" enemies through a "language of racism." As long as Americans believe that we are so different that we must consistently categorize ourselves based on false "racial" labels, then we will continue to base our decisions--often life or death decisions--on the confusing, arbitrary and deceptive notions of "race." The BOLD AMERICAN OUTLOOK is dedicated toward preventing American young people from continuing the tragic perpetuation of racism's legacy in the United States in their lives and beyond. This book is for those who are looking for a future-oriented and solutions-based focus for ending racism in the United States.

ACKNOWLEDGMENTS

I have so much to be thankful for and feel truly blessed to have been able to write this book. Of all my influences, besides those in my family, the greatest, without a doubt is Dr. Ashley Montagu, former professor of anthropology at Harvard, Princeton and Rutgers University among others and recipient of honorary awards and degrees from organizations and colleges around the world. A prolific and profound writer of many subjects, but by far his greatest work is *"Man's Most Dangerous Myth: The Fallacy of Race."* This is a book that really opened my eyes and gave me the motivation to continue my research and eventually write this book. To Dr. Montagu I am forever grateful. At this writing Dr. Montagu, in at age 94 is not in good health. My prayers and thoughts for his improved health are with him as I complete this book.

Others who have influenced me greatly include Michael Vannoy Adams, Maya Angelou, James Baldwin, Ruth Benedict, Jung Min Choi, David Theo Goldberg, Ian F. Haney-Lopez, Eric Mark Kramer, Don C. Locke, Stephen Molnar, Yehudi Webster and Cornel West.

I also want to thank and acknowledge members of my family, my mother Mary Evelyn; father, Joseph; my wife, Angela and the boys, Davin, Anthony and Andrew. My brothers and sisters, Dale, Frank, Linda and Monique for all their support. And all the other members of our families.

I want to thank Mr. Mark Davidson, my journalism professor at Calif. State University, Dominquez Hills for lighting a fire in me for social justice in whatever one writes. And a special thanks to all those at 5630 for their patience with me.

I also want to thank all those at 1stBooks and particularly Jennifer Orndorff for seeing this project through to completion – Thank You.

And most of all, I thank God, for allowing me to complete this book AND for making us all so culturally different and yet so much alike.

This Book is dedicated to:
My Loving Wife Angela
And our Sons
Davin, Anthony and Andrew

Contents

Introduction

"If Americans are to learn to deal with [find solutions for] racism in education, they will first need a point of view and we will need courage, for racism pervades this society like a cancer, eroding the humanity and capacity of all."

– Charles Wilson, "Racism in Education"

"Education can be a powerful force in the struggle to eliminate racism."

– Frances E. Kendall, "Diversity in the Classroom: A Multicultural Approach to the Education of Young Children"

As an American concerned about the future of this nation, the words of Charles Wilson above were like a call to action for me and a call for action for our country. I sincerely hope this book meets the challenge he puts before us. Not only is developing a point-of-view difficult, but implementing one will be even more difficult. I believe I have done my part by creating what I think is a viable and capable solution to racism's legacy in America. A point of view is not a simple thing to come by, but after years of thought and reflection I came to the conclusion that the BOLD AMERICAN OUTLOOK is right for the future of America and for the future of America's young people.

After reading this handbook, I challenge you to do your part by having the courage to implement a BOLD AMERICAN OUTLOOK among the American young people in your schools, classroom or home. In doing so, I sincerely believe that we can play a huge part in eliminating the cancer of racism in our young people's lifetime. This cancer may not consume adult Americans today, but its historical momentum may well consume the innocent lives of our young people if we allow racism's legacy to continue.

The BOLD AMERICAN OUTLOOK, A New Post-Racism Paradigm™ for the 21st Century, is unprecedented in its scope and its possibilities to change how you think and more importantly how America's young people think about themselves and others. An exciting aspect of this change to a post-racism paradigm is that the end result will be improved human relations between all Americans and particularly America's young people. The purpose of this book is to help you show American young people how they can be the first generations of Americans to effectively end racism's legacy in their lifetime.

This is the first book designed and written entirely from a viewpoint that seeks to empower young people, as they mature to adulthood, to disengage and defuse racism's legacy in America's future. The BOLD AMERICAN OUTLOOK can and WILL do this with your help. As an educator or parent concerned about the continuing presence of racism's legacy, you can play an unprecedented role in the beginning of the end of racism in America. Your dedication toward instilling the BOLD AMERICAN OUTLOOK Principles detailed in Chapter 3 and in teaching your student/child the importance of avoiding the 'language of racism' – the various words and concepts of 'race' 'color' and 'minority' status will, over time, give young people the conceptual tools they need to move beyond the deceptive paradoxes of 'race' and toward effective solutions to racism's legacy.

The BOLD AMERICAN OUTLOOK also emphatically furthers the view that racism is a historical construct that is only perpetuated by the various words and concepts of 'race' 'color' and 'minority' status within the American discourse. This is not to say that the BOLD AMERICAN OUTLOOK teaches that racism does not exist – it certainly does, because the 'language of racism' is still prevalent. Yet, the BOLD AMERICAN OUTLOOK teaches that racism's legacy only exist within the minds and beliefs of those who continue to use the old-world 'language of racism' within American social, educational, scientific, economic and political institutions. All else, including many things we now associate with 'racism' such as 'hate crimes' are simply what they are. Rude behavior, criminal or deviate behavior or violence should be dealt with appropriately for what they are (and perhaps more harshly and fairly) and not be given the politicized labels of 'hate crimes' or 'racism.'

The purpose of the BOLD AMERICAN OUTLOOK is to help educators and parents teach young people, within American schools or homes, that the concepts of 'race' 'color' and 'minority' status are all false human identities. MOREOVER, the continued use of these terms perpetuate a lie that this nation has too long condoned – that there are 'races' of humans.

In short, there cannot be racism if indeed there are no 'races.' And, the reality is that there are NO 'races.' An additional intent of this book is to provide the valuable information I've gathered from years of research to show a concerned adult or educator, how to teach your children or your students how to avoid inheriting and transmitting America's most enduring social cancer – racism's legacy.

You will notice throughout this book that the various words associated with 'race' and 'color' i.e., 'racial' or 'racist' or 'black' and 'white' etc, and the term 'minority' will always be in quotes. This is intentional on my part because I want to convey to the reader that these terms are indeed so-called – they have no basis in fact or reality. Also, note that I consistently refer to racism as 'racism's legacy' and that racism alone is never in quotes because racism, unlike 'race' is an historical fact. You will learn later why you must always refer to racism as racism's legacy.

The United States, even with all its faults is a great country to live in and I am very proud to be an American citizen. Yet, it is the BOLD AMERICAN OUTLOOK's stated belief that far too much focus is placed on American history in regard to racism today. I firmly believe in the vitality of American history as a foundation to build upon. It is upon this foundation of American history, of which I am forever a fond student, that I base my firm belief that *the historical momentum of racism's legacy* – and the life we breathe into it with the 'language of racism' – is the greatest threat to the survival of this nation, more than any outside our borders.

A crucial aspect of racism's legacy in America is the perpetuated belief that there are such things as 'races' within the United States and that there are 'colored' people, particularly the oft mentioned and so-called 'black' and so-called 'white' people. The longer that such beliefs and ignorance exist – which origins date back centuries – the greater the possibility that there will be a 'race' war between the dreaded and imagined 'black' and 'white' people. Principally because we really believe that 'races' and 'colored' people really exist.

We Americans will have our own 'ethnic cleansing' but ours will be far worse and not only for all the innocent lives that will be lost – the prelude is in our midst – but more so because our 'ethnic cleansing' is more about imagined identities and less about ethnicity. For the concepts of 'races' of Americans are not based in fact or human reality, they are essentially myths.

'Race' and racism are nothing we should concern ourselves with as far as our social reality is concerned. We can do far more by concerning ourselves with ridding from the American discourse the very words and concepts that divert us and inhibit us from getting to the root of our very real individual and social problems. It is not entirely adults who must change our discourses, but it is a matter of us, adults, teaching our young people the <u>process</u> of not using the 'language of racism' in their future discourses.

The BOLD AMERICAN OUTLOOK's Mission Statement is simply this:

To expose the 'language of racism' – the various words and concepts of 'race' 'color' and 'minority' status – within

the American written and oral discourse for what it truly is:
The delivery system for the perpetuation of racism's
legacy. This 'language of racism' also works to polarize
and divide Americans unnecessarily and tragically. The
BOLD AMERICAN OUTLOOK's Mission is to instill within
all American young people a 'post-racism paradigm' that
allows them to focus on solutions while rejecting the old
paradigms of 'racial' and 'minority' identities.

I am under no illusions that the great majority of adults and educators who read or hear of the BOLD AMERICAN OUTLOOK will embrace it and champion its vision. Yet, I do hope that most will understand that racism's legacy is still a very serious problem for this nation because of its perpetuation in our discourses. And, I hope adults today can understand and accept the fact that because of its historical momentum, racism's legacy will not likely end in your lifetime. Yet, if this new and unprecedented paradigm, the BOLD AMERICAN OUTLOOK, is implemented in schools district-wide, and it is hoped, eventually nation-wide, then there is a good chance racism's legacy will end in our children's lifetime.

When I began the BOLD AMERICAN OUTLOOK, I began to see that if we sincerely want to end racism's legacy we cannot simply trust that omitting a few words from our vocabulary, and remembering a few principles would bring about any effective change. What was also needed was something to focus on that conveys an American ideal, an ideal for courage and a vision or outlook on life for the good of all Americans. That's why I decided on the name, 'the BOLD AMERICAN OUTLOOK. It is the vision and point-of-view I believe Mr. Wilson was speaking of, and concurs with Mr. Appiah's quote at the top of Chapter 1 and Mr. Baldwin's at the top of my Logical Conclusion. **What America needs is a BOLD vision** to end racism's legacy today and into the future. I think that the BOLD AMERICAN OUTLOOK will help to that end.

Lastly, the reader MUST understand that drastic measures must be taken to stem the ongoing rush of racism's legacy and its historical momentum.   This can never be underestimated, if we indeed seek to rid our nation of the cancer of racism's legacy. I trust you will see, as you read this handbook, that the BOLD AMERICAN OUTLOOK is the most viable and promising paradigm for the future health of the United States and for ending racism's legacy in our young people's lifetime.

Chapter 1 What is the BOLD AMERICAN OUTLOOK?

"The proper response to Eurocentrism is surely not a reactive Afrocentrism, but a new understanding that humanizes all of us by learning to think beyond race."

- K. Anthony Appiah, 1993. 1

The BOLD AMERICAN OUTLOOK is a solution-based educating _process_ and a 'post-racism paradigm' that allows young Americans to acquire the understanding, over time, that the 'language of racism' – the various words and concepts of 'race' 'color' and 'minority' status toward humans in the American discourse – is not in their best interest as they mature into the 21st century.

The BOLD AMERICAN OUTLOOK will also help young people to understand that this 'language of racism' not only perpetuates racism's legacy, but is also harmful to their ability to relate with their fellow Americans in the future. Moreover, I emphasize _process_ above because the fight against racism's legacy must indeed be a process. A process that involves years of instilling a 'post-racism paradigm' into the hearts and minds of American young people. The facts are that 'races' and 'colored' people and 'minority' people do not exist as human realities.

Yet, the exclusion of a few key words is not all that is needed. Just as importantly, the BOLD AMERICAN OUTLOOK strongly urges educators/parents to also implement the BOLD AMERICAN OUTLOOK Principles consisting of three key principles: Courage, Fairness and Cultural Respect when teaching young people how to alter their thinking, writing and speaking about racism's legacy. Also the BOLD AMERICAN OUTLOOK stresses that all American individuals have a CULTURAL essence and NOT a 'racial' one.

Essentially, the BOLD AMERICAN OUTLOOK is a new vision and 'post-racism paradigm'™ for the future of the United States designed specifically for young Americans. A 'post-racism paradigm' – a mode of thinking that rejects 'race' 'color' and 'minority' status toward humans – will prevent America's young people from making the same mistakes adults today and those before us have made. That mistake is being unaware of how the 'language of racism' acts as the delivery system for the perpetuation of racism's legacy and as a camouflage for our true social and individual ills.

A BOLD AMERICAN OUTLOOK refuses to allow America's young people to recognize beliefs or concepts that imply or state directly that there are such things as 'black' people, 'white' people, 'minority' people, 'people of color' and people of a certain 'race' or 'races.' Persons holding such beliefs are only perpetuating the old-world paradigms and wrong idea of fixed 'races' which denies the great majority of Americans their right and freedom to honor and be identified by their true cultural heritages and American heritage.

The BOLD AMERICAN OUTLOOK is not a curriculum-based program and does not claim any sort of ethnocentric agenda. It does not make any rules or assumptions as far as how a school district, school or teacher prepares any course or study process. All that the BOLD AMERICAN OUTLOOK demands is what our young people deserve – an unbiased and accurate account of human identity in an education environment. In this respect, the BOLD AMERICAN OUTLOOK strongly urges that educators/parents interject (or encourage their students to interject) the BOLD AMERICAN OUTLOOK principles whenever the various words or concepts of 'race' 'color' or 'minority' status arise within a course or class discussion once students are familiar with The BOLD AMERICAN OUTLOOK. This will allow enhanced discussions and thinking without having to throw out current student text or study materials. Indeed, these materials are needed to show young people by example how – even up to the present – that the old paradigms of labeling people by 'race' and 'color' still exist.

It is not the BOLD AMERICAN OUTLOOK's intent to teach young people to reject, entirely, current or historical texts. The intent is to educate young people on how to reject certain parts of current or past texts that use words and concepts that distort accurate human identity, and thus, inhibiting their ability to reason.

3

Young Americans will learn, with the help of understanding educators/parents that 'race' and 'color' identities are not natural or given aspect of their lives, but are entirely human-made constructs and are historical constructs that they indeed have control over. An unfortunate side effect of racism's legacy today is that many of today's adults and indeed most teen-agers actually believe in or have internalized their false 'racial' identity. And as a consequence many adults believe that they have no control over their personal identity. We must not allow our young people to be socialized in this way. Young people must be taught that they do have control over their identity if it indeed has anything to do with their cultural identity or ancestry.

The reality is that we are not born into a 'race,' we were all assigned a 'race' centuries ago by individuals and institutions who actually knew very little about human variability but had obsessive desires to classify humans by a person's 'exterior look' or phenotype. We all learn that we must not judge a book by its cover and to judge a person by their 'exterior cover' is far worse. Today we merely repeat or perpetuate the old-world paradigms of what humans are. We are, in fact, living in a "time warp" in regards to how we identity humans today and the identity we accept and internalized for ourselves.

The BOLD AMERICAN OUTLOOK also strongly urges you to teach young people to reject any idea or claim to the superiority of any cultural group. This includes past and present suggestions that some cultures are 'primitive.' We must further the fact that all cultures are relative and in essence equal and essential to their particular environment or geographical location.

Cultures develop according to their own terms and needs. Though some cultures appear to be more sophisticated and complex than others, some are not as sophisticated primarily because they choose not to be, relative to their time and space as a culture. Likewise, for some cultures the survival of their traditional customs and culture are more important than developing a sophisticated or complex culture.

The overall aim of the BOLD AMERICAN OUTLOOK is to instill within America's young people the COURAGE to confront and reject the still prevalent false concepts of 'races,' 'color' and 'minority' status toward humans. America's young people must also be taught to recognize the reality of our similarities as one human species while understanding the reality of our varied and sometimes complex cultural differences.

The single most important aspect of the BOLD AMERICAN OUTLOOK is its potential to rebuild the human spirit. It proposes to do so by encouraging American young people to practice Fairness toward all Americans. Just as important, they must practice Cultural Respect by embracing and celebrating the cultural heritages of their fellow Americans. I elaborate further on these two BOLD AMERICAN OUTLOOK Principles in Chapter Three.

In closing, as we move into the 21st Century, I cannot emphasize enough the importance of a BOLD AMERICAN OUTLOOK for the future of this nation and America's young people. What the BOLD AMERICAN OUTLOOK proposes to accomplish is vital for America's multicultural future and for reaffirming the United States position as a model for peace and world leadership in the coming millennium.

1 – Appiah, K. Anthony, "Europe Upside Down: Fallacies of the New Afrocentrism." From Times Literary Supplement (Feb. 12th, 1993).

Chapter 2 Why is the BOLD AMERICAN OUTLOOK Needed?

"The safe solutions of the past would not be sufficient for solving the dangerous problems of the present."
— Abraham Lincoln 1

   "As long as racial reasoning regulates thought and action [in America], racism will continue to haunt America . . .. The fundamental aim is to replace racial reasoning with moral reasoning and understand that this is not an affair of skin pigmentation, but rather a matter of ethical principles."
— to paraphrase Cornel West "Race Matters"

There is a need for the BOLD AMERICAN OUTLOOK today because America's young people are confused about racism's legacy in the United States and do not know how to even begin the process of ending racism's legacy, let alone talk about it. *The BOLD AMERICAN OUTLOOK Handbook – A New Post-Racism Paradigm™ for the 21ˢᵗ Century* will not only give young people a new way of talking about racism's legacy – past and present – but it will also give them a new way of thinking about solutions to racism's legacy as they mature. This new way of thinking will become evident because the current paradigms of 'race' and 'color' toward human identity inhibit our ability today to reason and think logically when discussing America's most enduring and tragic social cancer.

A BOLD AMERICAN OUTLOOK will do this by placing a greater focus on solutions without using the archaic and false 'language of racism' – the various words and concepts of 'race,' 'color' and 'minority' status – and by encouraging incentives for young people who apply the BOLD AMERICAN OUTLOOK Principles (see Chapter 3) in their school work and life outlook.

To my knowledge, in regards to school-based policies, no school district anywhere has been BOLD enough to do what the BOLD AMERICAN OUTLOOK intends to do for you and your students. With the BOLD AMERICAN OUTLOOK as your conceptual vision and guide, and your school district as your support; you will be able to eliminate the concepts, ideas and notions of 'white' people, 'black' people, 'minorities' ' people of color' and 'races' of people as you instruct your students. Though not a simple process, the elimination of these 'categories' of Americans is essential for preventing American young people from perpetuating racism's legacy – and all the pitfalls and misrepresentations that come with this legacy – as they mature to adulthood.

The reasons for eliminating these concepts are simple: 'races' or 'people of color' – including so-called 'whites' who are left out of <u>this</u> 'concept,' simply do not exist. These 'racialized' concepts only lead to errors of logic and reason that confuse and incite tensions. So-called 'races' and 'colored' people are all figments of our social imaginations and upbringing. 'Racial' identities are arbitrary. These socially constructed identities or classifications change at a whim, depending on where you live or whom you talk to.

The 'racial' classification of humans will only end only when the generations of Americans who are raised using a 'post-racism paradigm' like the BOLD AMERICAN OUTLOOK Principles mature into adulthood and change the current institutional policies that further 'racial' categories.

The BOLD AMERICAN OUTLOOK's primary goal is to allow young people to understand that the various words and concepts of 'race' 'color' and 'minority' status toward humans actually work to perpetuate racism's legacy. An equally important goal is to show YOU, the concerned educator or parent that, this is true. It is essential that YOU teach this to your children and students and educate them to the benefits of stressing an individual's unique and complex cultural essence and not the simplistic and erroneous 'racial' essence.

Another reason that the BOLD AMERICAN OUTLOOK is needed is because there are no school/home-based paradigms out there that are primarily designed toward getting young people to focus on solutions to racism's legacy. Most so-called 'race' relation or cultural diversity programs today focus on erroneous historic constructs of human identity or historical 'racial' issues or even on present-day issues. Many of the so-called 'race' relations camps focus on teen-agers who have already internalized our societies 'racial' concepts and most of the young people only end up rehashing familiar attitudes and stereotypes that leave little time to discuss real solutions. Subsequently, all of these programs have led to no substantial progress. The evidence to this is obvious. The great majority of adults and educators claim that efforts to end racism's legacy have gone nowhere, and many claim that things have actually gotten worse.

The BOLD AMERICAN OUTLOOK proposes to be a BOLD and fresh new vision for the future of today's young people by focusing on solutions through a 'post-racism paradigm' that rejects the old paradigms of 'race' and 'color'. It is THE point of view that America's young people will need as they mature into the new millennium.

We should never give American young people any reason to believe that 'race' is some old fact that just exist, without any means for <u>them</u> do anything about it when they mature into adults. It is my firm belief that any child that matures with a BOLD AMERICAN OUTLOOK will readily understand how to use the historical nature of racism's legacy as a foundation to build a personal character that's strong enough to combat the inevitable onslaught of the historical momentum of racism's legacy. With the addition of the BOLD AMERICAN OUTLOOK Principles: COURAGE, FAIRNESS and CULTURAL RESPECT, detailed in the next chapter, any American young person will have the means to make their future more meaningful and the United States a better place to live.

1-"Class, Culture and Race in American Schools" Rothstein, Stanley – 1995
2 – Cornel West, "Race Matters" – 1993.

Chapter 3 The BOLD AMERICAN OUTLOOK Principles

"As long as a people believe in absurdities, they will continue to commit atrocities."

– Voltaire.

The BOLD AMERICAN OUTLOOK adamantly encourages the use of three key life principles: Courage, Fairness and Cultural Respect while teaching the BOLD AMERICAN OUTLOOK or during discussions with young people concerning the 'language of racism' or racism's legacy. Perhaps more than the awareness of the detrimental effects of the 'language of racism,' these three principles will greatly enhance the effectiveness of the BOLD AMERICAN OUTLOOK for young people in relation to racism's legacy and in relation to WHO they are and WHAT they can become.

COURAGE

Courage is a vital and necessary asset for any person, adult or child, yet it is especially important for educators/parents to stress this key virtue when discussing how to end the 'language of racism' and racism's legacy, particularly at an early age. In fact, I believe that it is precisely a lack of courage – by good people – that allow for the absurdities to continue and thus the inevitable atrocities that Voltaire speaks of above.

American educator, actress, director and writer Maya Angelou, once stated: **"Courage is the most important of all virtues because without courage one cannot practice any other virtue with consistency. You cannot be consistently kind, fair, just or generous without courage."** These words have many deep and profound implications toward our American dilemmas today and not just toward ridding ourselves from racism's legacy. As Ms. Angelou so eloquently states, we must have the courage to be kind to one another, to be fair – more on this later – to be just toward one another and to be generous and giving toward others.

These things may not seem to have anything to do with racism's legacy yet they do. All of these are consistently misrepresented with claims or accusations of racism, when the reality is we are simply what we show to one another. We show: a lack of kindness toward our fellow Americans; a lack of fairness toward our fellow Americans; a lack of justice toward our fellow Americans; and a lack of generosity toward our fellow Americans. <u>Above all</u>, we must honestly admit, <u>we often show a lack of courage</u>.

And we not only think our young people don't notice it. We also think our young people don't learn this lack of courage. At least, we think that they don't learn it from us. We think they learned it from someone else. Well, think again. We MUST refocus our teaching of courage to American young people and teaching it along the lines of empowering them to eradicate racism's legacy in the United States is the best possible means of doing so. Racism's legacy is a problem that young people did not initiate, yet they must deal with it and what we adults don't seem to comprehend is that racism's legacy not only confounds and frustrates young people, its historical momentum has a snowballing effect that eventually crushes their spirit and courage to live by the time they reach high school.

Young people, especially teen-agers, can sense the cancer that's eating away at social relations in this nation, but can't really verbalize what it is, or they're not sure if racism' legacy has anything to do with it. Some can actually verbalize that something is terribly wrong with this nation and some lash out in an attempt to release their frustrations over not being able to do anything about it because they don't know how.

The great thing about the BOLD AMERICAN OUTLOOK is that it actually empowers young people to begin to do something about a social problem that they believed only grown-ups could resolve. The BOLD AMERICAN OUTLOOK's expressed intent is to get America's young people thinking about how they can first understand, then control and eventually end racism's legacy as they mature. This is something they will really cherish for the BOLD AMERICAN OUTLOOK will give them the distinction of being the first generation of Americans to effectively begin the end of racism's legacy in the United States.

It pains me to bring it up, but the reality is that the young men responsible for the massacre at Columbine High School did not have a sense of control or courage in their lives and thus decided to control the fate of others through an extreme lack of courage. One of the teen-agers, the reported leader of the two, also had expressed in writings, distorted 'racial' views before they went on their rampage. It takes courage to live through all the pains and discomforts of teen-age angst, yet these young men did not have the courage to do so. It is not entirely unlikely that they were never consistently taught to have the courage to persevere and to be kind, fair, just and generous from an early age. One thing we do know, they did inherit our old-world views and distorted beliefs on 'race' and these views may well have distorted their own views on life's possibilities.

We adults, I believe, often take courage for granted and believe that only certain young people can possess it. We seem to believe that it is an endowed trait and that only fate comes into play when we see it evident in some young people. I sincerely believe that courage can be taught and I sincerely believe that you – the educator or parent – can teach it if you sincerely want to and sincerely make the effort. The process of teaching courage simply begins by recognizing that it is a process that takes years to develop. Much like the BOLD AMERICAN OUTLOOK itself, you must first begin to tell young people what it is and why it is important. You MUST begin by telling young people that courage is the most important virtue they will ever possess and that it applies to virtually all other aspects of their lives. Teaching young people to have the courage to stand up and reject the old paradigms that embody thinking of people as 'races' 'colored' or 'minorities' can be a perfect starting point for showing young people the importance of courage that can be beneficial to them and others for a lifetime.

I cannot emphasize enough how important it is to consistently instill the importance of having courage to American young people. This is the overwhelming reason why COURAGE is the first principle one needs to have a BOLD AMERICAN OUTLOOK.

FAIRNESS

The BOLD AMERICAN OUTLOOK is committed to instilling within American young people a strong sense of fairness toward everyone. Without fairness, as we all should remember from childhood, we instill a sense of bitterness in those who are treated unfairly. In addition, this can lead to more problems, sometimes worse than we could have imagined. For this reason alone, fairness must be firmly ingrained in America's young people if we want them to have a BOLD AMERICAN OUTLOOK.

"Fairness toward other groups or a person is a matter of simple human decency; and decency is an attitude of mind, for the most part culturally conditioned," states Ashley Montagu in "Man' Most Dangerous Myth." Yet, there are other variables involved with fairness that we should examine. Montagu goes on to say that, "The plea for fairness for ethnic groups not our own is usually phrased in terms of 'tolerance.' But if we are to make progress in ethnic relations, it is desirable to recognize that tolerance is not good enough.

"Tolerance is the attitude of those who consider themselves not only different but superior . . . We must be more than tolerant; we must be fair. Tolerance is the best we can hope for from bigots; fairness is the attitude of mind we look for in decent, humane people . . . One is called to be fair – to understand and then act upon that understanding. Until such an attitude of mind becomes part of the equipment of every individual, no amount of instruction in the facts concerning the biology of race will ever succeed in eliminating race prejudices."[1]

If we look at fairness historically, we can see that though it has long been an American ideal, it has rarely been meted out equally among all Americans. In fact, the lack of fairness can be said to be a vital for allowing the roots of racism to prosper in the United States.

We must also understand though that though fairness has implications with racism's legacy, fairness, in and of itself, can be a singular virtue that we must all strive for. In other words, you don't necessarily have to think of being fair just because of racism's legacy, but one may use fairness as a catalyst for change if one perceives that racism's legacy is being perpetuated.

As an American of visibly African ancestry, I have often spoken to and heard many Americans who look like me state that, "Hey, I don't care what they call me, I don't care what the say. As long as they treat me fairly, I'm okay with that." This is a similar refrain that is also heard in regard to cultural respect – which I'll get too later – as well. "As long as you show me respect, I'm fine with that."

In conclusion on fairness, Amy Gutmann eloquently summed up our moral duty toward instilling this principle into the American ethos: "Fairness, not colorblindness, is the fundamental principle of justice by which policies must be judged in the non-ideal world." 2

CULTURAL RESPECT

Though last, Cultural Respect is certainly not least in importance among the BOLD AMERICAN OUTLOOK Principles. Not surprisingly though, Cultural Respect is often overlooked when claims of racism are made and even in historical volumes on racism's legacy. The reasons are clear. First, accurate cultural recognition is rarely used and historical records have consistently used 'race' or 'color' descriptors and thus they became the 'standard' manner of identifying Americans historically.

African-Americans became 'blacks'; European-Americans became 'whites'; Native American nations/population groups simply became 'Indians' though some were given recognition of their nation or 'tribal' name. Also, historically in the United States Native American were called 'red' people. The various Asian-Americans were called 'yellow' people and the various Latino-Americans, particularly Mexican-Americans were called 'brown' people and have called themselves 'brown' to describe their culture, much like African-Americans continue to use 'black.'

Though some adults may recognized that terms of 'color' such as 'black,' 'brown,' 'yellow,' and 'red' have been used to deny various culture groups the proper recognition of their cultural heritage and dignity, an equally disturbing denial was at work.

Those we call 'whites' – European-Americans – have also been denied the proper recognition of their various cultural heritages. Though there is some political reasons that become evident that makes this term difficult to abandon, it too must be eliminated and the reason is not to end the so-called 'white' majority.

As simply 'whites,' European-Americans lose much more than the obvious absence of their true cultural identity. These lose critical connections to American that may or may not be related to them but who may indeed share one of their cultural heritages. The absence of information about one's cultural heritage can be both profound and tragic.

Daily, millions of Americans, particularly so-called 'white' Americans and so-called 'black' Americans pass each other without even looking each other in the eye, let alone thinking that one or the other may be related to each other but the probability is much higher than you might think. In her book, "The Sweeter the Juice – A Family Memoir in Black and White" Shirlee Taylor Haizlip, an American of African ancestry who looks 'white' states that, "Geneticist have said that 95% of 'white' Americans have widely varying degrees of 'black' ancestry. According to: *The Source: A Guidebook to American Genealogy*, 75% of all African-Americans have at least one 'white' ancestor and 15% have predominantly 'white' [heritage]. **The fact that biologist continue to glean these truths from their study of genetic data gives weight to the claim that there are no 'real white Americans.'** As Adrian Piper wrote, the longer a person's family has lived in this country, the higher the probable percentage of African ancestry . . .."3

There have been many other like studies that have revealed that the so-called 'whites' and 'blacks' are much more likely to be related than other American culture groups. But the overarching fact is this: we are all Americans and we just as soon rid ourselves of the absurd practice of identifying ourselves by 'race' or 'color.'

The BOLD AMERICAN OUTLOOK strongly urges educators and parents to teach young people to begin to get into the practice of replacing any written use of the various words associated to 'race' or 'color' or 'minority' term with the word American. Then re-read the article or passage and try to make sense of it. Remember that the true identity of each of the persons identified is American more often than not – besides if a person is an immigrant that notation is usually made evident in some manner. The reader will soon realize that the originally written piece only included the 'race' or 'minority' status of those involved as a means of evoking some kind of emotion within the reader. In most cases, you will discover that the article or passage has no logical purpose without the 'race' 'color' or 'minority' status of the persons involved.

The reason for this is made clear by Michael Vannoy Adams in "The Multicultural Imagination." Adams states that, "The reason categories like 'color' are so useless is that they convey very little, in any, information about significant psychical differences . . . it is the 'low informational value' of a category like color that enables racist to endow it with a high projective value. The relative poverty of color allows it to be used – and abused – by racist who empower it with a wealth of significance and project uncritically." 4

This is not to say that there was no purpose for what was written, but moreover to recognize that in many cases the writer uses or manipulates a person's 'race' or 'minority' status as a crutch to support biased, stereotypical or 'racial' views that the writer expects you to accept. Particularly since most Americans rarely if ever reject or complain about the use of a person's 'racial' or 'minority' status in written literature or within the American discourse.

The BOLD AMERICAN OUTLOOK intends to help teach America's young people to avoid the use of 'race' 'color' and 'minority' identities because the use of an individual's CULTURAL heritage or ancestry is much more respectful of one's cultural identity and dignity – something all Americans are worthy of.

It is hoped that the reader can now understands that the BOLD AMERICAN OUTLOOK Principles are positive virtues for any young person nurture as they mature into adulthood. Moreover, I have faith and trust that there are at least a few responsible and concerned adult Americans across this land who understand that the BOLD AMERICAN OUTLOOK Principles are the kind of qualities that they indeed want to instill in their students/children.

It is my sincere hope that the BOLD AMERICAN OUTLOOK will be used as the point-of-view or vehicle that facilitates the furthering of these principles into the hearts and minds of America's young people. If anything, their future and the future of the United States will be a more healthy and hospitable one.

1 – Montagu, Ashley, "Man's Most Dangerous Myth" – 1964.

2 – Gutmann, Amy, "Color Consciousness" w/ K.Anthony Appiah – 1996.

3 – Haizlip, Shirlee Taylor, "The Sweeter the Juice" – 1996.

4 – Adams, Michael Vannoy, "The Multicultural Imagination" – 1996.

Chapter 4 The 'Language of Racism'

"The words we use to describe groups of people have developed within the system of racism as it has changed historically . . . We need to pay attention to the words we use because language itself is used to maintain racism."
– Paul Kivel, "Uprooting Racism"

The 'Language of Racism'™ is a term that I originated explicitly for the BOLD AMERICAN OUTLOOK to help explain how the various words and concepts of 'race' 'color' and 'minority' status are the delivery system for the perpetuation of racism's legacy. The major components – the root words for the 'language of racism' – are 'race' 'color' and 'minority' status. From these words come the words that allow for the reification of 'racial' and 'color' terms and the perpetuation of the 'minority' status of only certain American culture groups.

Here I will elaborate on the fallacies of 'race' 'color' and minority' – the root words of the 'language of racism.'

The Fallacy of 'Race'

'Race' is common-sense notion. It falls apart under rational scrutiny'
- David Lionel Smith, "The House that Race Built"

"Racially defined problems, by definition, cannot be resolved."
— Yehudi Webster- 1997

There are no 'races' of humans. In fact, only those who have used and continue to use this misnomer for human identity give currency to this bankrupt concept. The false concept of 'race' once had a significant, though absurd morally abject usefulness about it – when it was used to forge slavery in the United States and for Jim Crow laws. As Winant and Omi noted, "In the United States, the racial category of 'black' evolved with the consolidation of racial slavery. By the end of the 17th century, Africans, whose specific identity was Ibo, Yoruba, Falani, etc., were rendered 'black' by an ideology of exploitation based on racial logic – the establishment of the 'color line.'"

What was more remarkable here as Lerone Bennet, Jr. also pointed out in "Before the Mayflower" is that at this point in colonial, pre-American history, not only was a 'black racial' identity forged. Something else, a kind of justification of human 'blackness' also occurred. Winant and Omi state that, "With slavery, a racially based understanding of society was set in motion which resulted in the shaping of a specific 'racial' identity not only for the slaves but for the European settlers as well. Winthrop Jordan [author of "White over Black: American Attitudes Toward the Negro 1550-1812"] observed: From the initially common term 'Christian' at mid-century there was a marked shift . . . After about 1680, taking the colonies as a whole, a new term of self-identification appeared – 'white.'"

The validity and value of the belief in 'race' and 'races' is only as great as our use of the term. Not surprisingly, in the United States, the words and concepts of 'race' have accumulated a very high value indeed. But from now on that must change. It is incumbent upon us as responsible adults to eliminate entirely the value of 'race' to our young people and within the American discourse.

Those who teach young people with a BOLD AMERICAN OUTLOOK, must educate young people to fully understand that the various words and concepts of 'race' are wrong, invalid, empty of any positive meaning and bankrupt of any real value. In essence, young people must be taught to reject or avoid any usage of words associated with 'race.' And, we must teach young people that the concept of 'race' will no longer have currency in their future.

Moreover, the various words and concepts of 'race' are highly manipulative. So-called 'racial' terms have been used and abused not only by European-Americans, but all Americans, including to a great extent by those who share my cultural phenotype – African-Americans. The great majority of all Americans have so internalized the concepts of 'race' that most of us believe that it's a true human reality and don't dare contest the validity of 'race' – particularly African-Americans because we are, supposedly, striving to improve our 'race' – for fear of being a 'reverse-racist.'

Here is the greatest fallacy of 'race,' its vulnerability to be manipulated by whoever wants to manipulate it. So-called 'blacks' accusing so-called 'whites' of being 'racist' or vice versa; 'reverse discrimination'; the concepts of 'mixed race' 'interracial' or 'bi-racial'; 'multiracial'; 'race-baiting'; 'race-based'; and playing the 'race' card. All of these DEMAND one thing. That you believe in the concepts of 'race' and that there are 'races' of people.

The Fallacy of 'Color'

"Color is not a human or personal reality. Color is a political reality.
-James Baldwin – "The Fire Next Time"

There are no 'Black' people and no 'White' people or 'people of color' in the United States.**1**(Davis, Webster, et. al**)** Yet, there are millions and millions of Americans and thousands of writers and leaders on human relations in America that will have you believe so. The various concepts of 'color' or 'colored' people is perhaps, more than 'race,' the most pervasive and abused absurdity to emerge from racism's legacy in the United States.

For this reason and obvious others, the BOLD AMERICAN OUTLOOK strongly encourages adults and educators to avoid using terms of 'color' toward humans whenever possible, and to teach young people to avoid and reject the use of 'color' terms to describe Americans. The only appropriate alternative titles for describing humans – if they are at all necessary – are descriptors that come closest to one's cultural heritage or ancestry.

'Color' descriptors only perpetuate old-world images, steeped in vagueness and a denial of one's cultural dignity. 'Color' terms toward humans also lead to errors of rational logic and reason, a lack of greater understanding, as well as ironic confusions of human identity and tragic misrepresentations.

Let me give you a hypothetical, yet likely, scenario. Imagine that a group of about 10 young people, who all just happen to European-American or so-called 'white' are sitting at the outdoor fast food stand on a busy street in Anytown, USA. They're all joking and having a good time. One in the group begins to pointing out certain cars as they approached that he likes and don't like. Suddenly, every one's involved, yelling out what cars they like or don't like. Unfortunately, as a part of picking certain cars from others, the colors of the cars' are used by most.

Eventually, and a car approaches driven by Jamal and his friends. They're on their way to this same eatery. Jamal, happens to be African-American, but has been raised to believe that he is only 'black.' He was <u>not</u> taught that he was a proud American, descended from a proud African culture. Moreover, he was not taught that he was NOT 'black.' No he was just 'black.' This is what his parents were taught as young people, and they simply taught their son to "Say it Loud, I'm 'Black' and I'm Proud!" as the 1970's song by James Brown went. Also, Jamal's car just happens to be black and he just happens to have been having a very bad day, AND, he just happens to have a concealed automatic weapon in his car.

As he approaches the eatery and while turning into the parking lot, one in the group yells out, "I don't like that black one!" While pulling in, Luther hears the remark made by the teen. He turns toward the group again and sees that they are all laughing hysterically, because the teen who made the claim, immediately saw that the driver may have thought he was talking about the driver, since he quickly looked their way.

Jamal, unaware of what the loud laughter was about, seriously assumed that it must have been directed toward him <u>and for him that was the last straw</u>. He was not about to have his 'black' heritage ridiculed.

He reached under his seat and despite protest from friends in the car, he calmly walked over to the group of teens and shot seven or eight teens. The others ran off and avoided the barrage of bullets. Jamal then ran back to the car and drove off. The teen that made the remark was not shot.

Likely not to happen. We certainly hope so. Likely never to happen. We wish we can say so, but it is not entirely impossible. As long as any color that can be directed toward any non-human object or non-human animal, then the possibility for confusion or misrepresentations CAN happen. Likewise, any use of the word 'race' beyond the connotations of a contested event, also can lead to possible misrepresentations.

Now a real-life example. In a May 11, 1998 article in the Los Angeles Times, writer Sam Fulwood III reports on a controversy arising out of the discovery that the Meriam-Webster dictionary defines the word 'nigger' as: a 'black' person. Considering the historical baggage this word carries for African-Americans such as myself and American social relations, I can understand the unease with this definition. Yet, Americans in general and various African-Americans in particular, can move beyond such insensitive acts by first affirming the fact that no such thing as a 'black' person exist. Thus, the term 'nigger' is simply a historical epithet for what historically and ignorantly were known as 'black' people. There will then be no waste of time on historical baggage. No waste of emotion and energy which could be used toward finding solutions, such as questioning why the writer of the article constantly refers to African-Americans as 'black' in the article as if to confirm that we are only 'black' people.

In short, Americans are obsessed with the 'color' of their fellow Americans. Whether it's their naturally inherited melanin or a summer-time tan, Americans just can't seem to get enough of talking about the skin pigmentation of others.

There are valid reasons for this. The most obvious being that humans are visual beings. As we mature we learn to place a certain value on things or people based upon how we perceive or see them. For this reason it could be said that humans are *visiocentric* beings. **2(Kramer)** Unfortunately for Americans, this has some very serious side-effects.

As this nation matured, many of the leaders and founding fathers suddenly became color conscious. When the English settlers first arrived on the North American continent, they specifically identified themselves as

Englishmen or Christian. These settlers did not identify themselves as 'white' until the late 1600s. As Lerone Bennet, Jr. noted, "It appears from surviving evidence that the first [English] settlers had no concept of themselves as 'white' people. . . The word 'white' with its burden of arrogance and biological pride developed late in the century as a direct result of slavery and the organized debasement of [Africans]."

The Fallacy of a 'Minority'

The BOLD AMERICAN OUTLOOK holds the view that there are no selective 'minorities' in the United States. 'Minority' group status, though a relatively new have been equated to culture groups that are non-European in recent ancestry. What is lost in the equation to most is the nature in which 'minority' is defined in American life. We seem to ignore the fact that all Americans are 'minorities' and that the term 'minority' only has substance if there is indeed a 'majority' – there is not.

The reality is that the so-called 'majorities' in America are, in fact, a combination of European-American 'minorities.' These combination of 'minorities' only becomes a 'majority' when the non-reality aspect of 'color' is brought into the American discourse as a 'real' and commonly used social identity. The non-reality claim is that European-American 'minorities' are 'white.' This claim, this false claim of 'whiteness,' began in the late 17th century. 'Whiteness' has now become a tradition of difference and political convenience.

If we are to give our American young people a chance to end claims of racism and racism's legacy, then this tradition and convenience must come to an end. In fact, this convenience of 'color' and 'minority' status is actually an inconvenience in regards to how these terms incite frictions and polarizes Americans unnecessarily. They also further the beliefs in the reality of an fixed and immutable 'color' essence in human reality – a very 'tool of racism' that help to establish and legitimize racism's legacy.

In conclusion, the 'language of racism' is not a complex and extensive language. It consists of less than a few dozen words. Yet, those few words are so entrenched and pervasive in the American discourse that the weight they have on the American public is a burden we cannot too long bear. This burden has an historical momentum that could possibly destroy the future of this nation and the future of America's young people.

We MUST be bold enough to set a precedent for America's young people. We must not allow them to repeat the mistakes we have inherited through the 'language of racism.' We adults learned this language unwittingly, as young people, young impressionable people, unaware of how the racism's legacy feeds on itself. More importantly, we are now poised to continue the inheritance of racism's legacy. Racism has been well documented by many writers, scholars and social scientist to be a social cancer. How proud can you be as an American, a teacher and a parent – knowing what you now know – to pass down this cancer to your students and to your child. If at least for their sake, help to empower America's young people with the knowledge and means to end our shameful social legacy. Empower them with a BOLD AMERICAN OUTLOOK.

Chapter 5 The History Diversion Syndrome

"Racism is not like 'race' . . . It is a belief that can be studied only historically."
— Ruth Benedict *1*

"In order to garner healthy [human] relations, a complete rupture with the past is necessary."
- Jung Min Choi *2*

The intent of this chapter is to serve as words of caution to the seeming obsessive and persistent use of history and recent so-called 'racial' events ONLY when discussions of racism occur in schools or in the home. It is the expressed desire of the BOLD AMERICAN OUTLOOK to actively engage young people into thinking more about solutions toward ending racism's legacy in the future, both immediate and long-term.

Though many of us are not aware of it, there are intentional distractions that have historically and in the present-day that contribute to the lack of progress and improvement in human relations in the United States. The 'History Diversion Syndrome' is perhaps the most prevalent. The key component of the History Diversion Syndrome (HDS)™ is this: historically and to the present, far too much time is spent rehashing the history of racism when discussing racism, when much more time and focus should be on finding solutions and acting upon them.

Part of the reason for this is simple, as stated above by Ruth Benedict and here in another form, "Racism, like any dogma than cannot be scientifically demonstrated, must be studied historically." I found myself spending too much time talking and reading about the history of racism or racism's legacy. In fact, I've spent years reading books and articles on the history of racism to write this book. But I was fortunate to discover an important virtue from those years of research. The most prominent being that if a solutions to a problem is really needed, you must spend more time talking, thinking and acting toward solutions than focusing on the problem. You can only spend so much time talking about the past or a problem. Soon you must do something that's progressive else you're just treading water and any swimmer can tell you that you can only tread for so long, and unless you begin to move you're going to sink.

This pretty much sums up what's going on in the United States today in regards to our attempts to improve our human relations or cure our social cancer. We've been treading water for so long, we're sinking into an abyss of created by a vast absence of courage, fairness, and cultural respect, peppered with diversions, distractions, misrepresentations and misunderstanding.

A graphic example of the HDS, our inability to find solutions and the emptiness of the concept of 'race' is the "Dialogue on Race" proposed by President Clinton. Upon hearing of this preposterous idea by Mr. Clinton, I twice wrote to him and the staff in charge of his "Commission on Race." I explicitly noted, "A dialogue on 'race' is futile and doomed because 'race' is not a true human reality. What you must stress Mr. Clinton is a dialogue to eliminate 'race' as a human identity in the American discourse." Unfortunately, he either did not get my letters, or if he did, did not bother to respond. I did get a letter from one of his bureaucratic assistants thanking me for writing to the President about an issue that he deems very important.

I am deeply and sincerely saddened that the President or his staff did not heed my warning, for here is what transpired. Esteemed and self-professed experts on 'race' and 'race relations' strode into Washington, D.C. and sat before the President's commission. The great majority of these 'race' experts were older adult Americans, all rehashing the old history of racism, from their old experiences and the result was the same old thing. Mostly talk about the racism long ago and recent. Hardly any talk concerning solutions or the actions needed to bring about any solutions were reported, so it can be assumed that there was little talk on solutions as well. In the end, instead of reporting to the President that they had failed to accomplish anything, they all summarily agreed that what they and this nation needed was more 'dialogue.' Sadly, they all knew this when they began. Even sadder, was the complete waste of time and energy that occurred.

This failure by President Clinton's commission is indicative of what I'm very concerned about and you should be too. This is also why I'm writing this book. To let educators and the public know that there is a viable solution to racism's legacy and it is NOT a "Dialogue on Race" as proposed by President Clinton. The solution is the BOLD AMERICAN OUTLOOK. It will end the focus on history or recent 'racial' events and place the focus on a change in the American discourse, particularly for young people, because they are more likely than today's adults –

we MUST admit – to implement solutions on from a 'non-racialized' viewpoint.

Unfortunately, as the President's Commission on 'Race' graphically showed, older adult Americans are incapable – due to being raised and socialized with 'race' 'color' and 'minority' concepts – of conceiving rational and significant solutions to our American dilemma – the consistent perpetuation of racism's legacy.

It disturbs me to see many well-educated writers, scholars and leaders who are in-tuned to the dynamics of racism's legacy but fail to use their intelligence toward possible solutions. In this sense I'm speaking of American intellectuals and leaders of all cultural heritages who consistently whip out articles or speak detailing recent 'racial' incidents and writers who consistently write on the history of racism. There are now more than enough books about the history of racism in the United States, I personally know this from my many years of research and from the seemingly monthly book reviews on a book about racism that I've noticed over the past few years.

In informal studied that I've made on discussions on remedying racism's legacy, I've found that the part that history plays in these discussions is at least 60%, time spent on recent or present-day issues 30% and the time spent on possible solutions or finding solutions – no more than 10%. This is unacceptable and must be inverted for the simple reason that in most cases when people sit down and talk, or even stand up and talk about racism they generally want solutions. We must begin to recognize that talking about historical and even recent 'racial' event are only diversions from the goal – solutions – so that these problems do not occur again. In future discussions on how racism's legacy is effecting you, your school and your students, you MUST spend more than 60% of that time on possible solutions.

For example, a discussion can be planned for finding ways to encourage your students or your child to use the THREE key principles of the BOLD AMERICAN

OUTLOOK and the elimination of the 'language of racism' can be discussed for 60% of a meeting/discussion. The remaining 40% can be used to cite historical or recent events to support your view on why these solutions must be implemented. Also, it may be beneficial to note to all attendees that the goal is to have a <u>solution-based</u> discussion i.e., what must or should be done NOW or in the future. Old issues or recent events will be given limited discussion because they are, in essence, history and <u>cannot</u> be changed.

The whole point is to have a focus on solutions and that it's okay to use the history of racism or recent events, but just don't focus on them. History lessons, the President's Commission on 'Race' and my informal study have all shown what is likely to occur. That when the focus is on past events, long ago or recent, the result is either nothing gets done, events are romanticized or exaggerated, or more often than not, people get mad or madder at each other. As a Native-American student once stated, "There is a certain amount of anger that come from the past [U.S. history]. 3 We all should know also that very little positive or productive progress is ever made when one is angry.

What is also important to understand is what Karen A. Callaghan calls a "hierarchical racial discourse." While discussing a focus on history in movies such as Pocahontas, Callaghan notes that "Disney's decision to focus on a historical episode rather than contemporary people and issues also reinforces a hierarchical racial discourse. The Pocahontas story line is basically fiction with a few allusions to real persons participating in the 1607 encounters between Europeans and Native Americans. While an opportunity for education is lost, this is to be expected. Few films portray historical events accurately. However, when racial struggles are presented only in historical contexts, symbolically the message is: The problem is in the past, too bad about what happened, but what can be done about it now? How can people living today be held accountable for the actions that occurred hundreds of years ago?"

Callaghan also cites Ward Churchill comments on the film Dances With Wolves, "It's all in the past, so the story goes; regrettable, obviously, but comfortably out of reach." This 'it's-all-in-the-past' representation of oppression, Callaghan goes on to say, "Symbolically denies the myriad of policies and actions that have occurred since the 15th century to produce the existing American racial hierarchy. No matter how enlightened or sensitive revisionism may be, focus on historical events alone reinforces the discourse that current power arrangements are beyond the scope of human agency. If racial-ethnic struggles and inequities are understood as merely remnants of the past, then once again racism can be assumed to originate from a mysterious, abstract source, an inviolate ground over which persons can enact no influence or sway."

Here again is evidence of how the HDS denies or prevents adult Americans from finding or even thinking about solutions to racism's legacy. We MUST take steps to assure that this does not happen to America's young people as they mature into adulthood. A 'post-racism paradigm' like the BOLD AMERICAN OUTLOOK will assist America's young people in recognizing how diversions such as the HDS prevents them from doing what needs to be done to arrive at solutions to racism's legacy in their lifetime.

1-Benedict, Ruth, "Race, Science and Politics" 1943

2-Choi, Jung Min, "Racist Ontology, Inferiorization and Assimilation" from "Postmodernism and Race" – Eric Mark Kramer – 1997

3-Tatum, Beverly, "Why Are All the Black Kids Sitting Together in the Cafeteria" – 1997.

4-Callaghan, Karen A., "Symbolic Violence and Race" from "Postmodernism and Race."

Chapter 6 How the Idea of 'Hate Crimes' Perpetuates Racism's Legacy

". . . almost every crime is motivated by hate of one kind or another, every set of bones deserves equal protection under the laws."

— Richard Dooling.

The idea of a 'hate crime' is a perfect example of a social redundancy that can only emerge from a society reeling from the guilt and remnants of racism's legacy. Those who teach the BOLD AMERICAN OUTLOOK must educate and inform young people that 'hate crime' laws perpetuate racism's legacy and are not solutions to that legacy. In fact, when 'hate crimes' are associated with a victim's or aggressor's 'race' or 'color' then it has, in effect, perpetuated racism's legacy of socially constructing that person's legal or judicial expectations of benefits or burdens based on one's 'race' and 'color.' (Today's Supreme Court, by the way, is masterful at this form of Constitutional alchemy.)

Like 'affirmative action' the intent of 'hate crimes,' – to help American 'others' who are still 'racially' defined and political 'others' who are irrationally defined – is hopelessly flawed. Thus, only some Americans benefit from 'hate crime' logic and all Americans lose, because in the end, the concept of 'hate crime' ignores the reality that crime, all crimes, are acts that humans do to humans. What is needed is a focus on why humans commit crimes against fellow humans and NOT just certain humans.

Do you know when the term 'hate crime' was coined? Why can't a child or a woman be a victim of a 'hate crime'? Do 'hate crimes' make sense to you? Well, the answers are: 1985; because 'hate crimes' are arbitrary and political; and NO, they don't make rational sense.[1] More importantly, they help to perpetuate racism's legacy by furthering the false notions that there are 'black' victims, 'white' aggressors and 'minority' victims.

Ironically though, if you are gay or Jewish you can be a victim of a 'hate crime.' Which means that only a gay Jewish woman or a gay Jewish child can be a victim of 'hate crime.' If you are a non-gay woman or non-gay child, you cannot be a victim of a 'hate crime' because 'these' people are not protected by 'hate crime' legislation. Does any of this make sense? Furthermore, in the skewed logic of 'hate crimes' according to the Los Angeles County Commission on Human Rights, even 'white' people can be victims of a 'hate crime'! 2

So just what is a 'hate crime' then, if virtually everyone can be a victim of one, and yet, only certain people are?

Lets look at a recent example:

In a highly publicized crime, three men robbed and beat a man and then tied him to a rope and the back of their pickup truck and drove down a country road until the tie-up man's body came apart. Now this would be a horrendous act and crime to anyone who hears of it. Yet, only in the United States are the so-called 'race' and 'color' of the participants showcased. Here is how this crime was reported nation-wide: "Three white men are accused of dragging a black man down a country road from the back of their pickup truck . . . Prosecutors will seek to prosecute the men for a hate crime." As I write this, two of the so-called 'white' men have been convicted. The two convicted men, John William King and Lawrence Russell Brewer, were also connected to a so-called 'White' supremacist group while in prison years before the crime.

Now what we must do as responsible adults and educators is to look at these statements and ponder, why does the 'color' of the persons involved matter. Well the reasons are primarily historical and we perpetuate that history when we continue to use these 'color' terms unnecessarily.

Should not any person who kills another, except in self-defense or in a time of war, be subject to the ultimate penalty by law. Why should a penalty be greater or less if a victim or perpetrator have more or less melanin that the other? The answer to that is also in American history.

Historically in the United States persons of obvious European phenotype, and not obvious non-European ancestry, have not been accorded equal justice under the law when they committed a crime against a non-European-American or immigrant. Until recently, the great majority of these crimes were committed toward the various Native-

41

American groups, Asian-American groups, African-Americans and Mexican-Americans.

To correct these frequent miscarriages of justice, a bill was introduced in Congress in 1985 requiring the Justice Department to collect and publish statistics on the nature and number of crimes motivated by 'racial,' religious and ethnic prejudice. The sponsors of the bill coined it the 'hate crimes statistics' bill. At the same time, news stories told of how the nation was in the throes of an epidemic of 'hate crimes,' even before any statistics were collected.3

A Hate Born of Hate

By 1990 the Federal 'Hate Crimes Statistics Act' (HCSA) was passed. Jacobs and Potter note that, "The HCSA's most glaring omission was gender prejudice . . . It also ignored crimes against the mentally and physically disabled and children . . . Nothing can more poignantly demonstrate what we mean by the 'social construction of a hate crime.'"

Jacobs and Potter go on to state that the great majority of violent crimes, 80%, are committed by people of the same cultural group. They conclude that 'hate crime' legislation foments more hatred than it deters. The writers are convinced, as we should be, that almost every crime is motivated by hate of one kind or another.3

The lead paragraph of an article on August 26, 1999 by the Associated Press began: "A white man was beaten kicked in the head and left for dead with a rope around his neck on an Indian reservation. Three Indians were arrested."4 What is interesting about the article is the continued use of the false terms 'white' and 'Indian.' One has to wonder if the article would have even made the editor's cut of news to print that day if the so-called 'color' or 'Indian' status of those involved was not mentioned.

It does not take a great leap in logic to see that 'hate crimes,' as a social construction by American lawmakers, is but a remnant of our social constructions of 'race,' 'colored' people and 'minorities.' In essence, 'hate crimes' need these other distorted human identities to have any logic of their own. But in the end, their dependence on distortions of human reality, like 'race' and 'minorities, or even 'Indian' status, only hastens their irrationality, or as noted earlier, only produces more hatred.

The idea of a 'hate crime' also allows one or a group to mask their real criminal and violent natures. This is readily evident in respect to so-called 'white' supremacist.If one believes that he/she is a 'white' supremacist and goes out and commit a criminal or violent act under the guise of their 'white' supremacist beliefs. These beliefs include that there are 'black' people and other 'non-white' people who are all inferior to 'white' people. Thus, so-called 'white' supremacist feel justified in their actions and beliefs because the majority of Americans agree with their belief in their 'whiteness' – we don't deny it. Also, we don't call them what they really are – mentally disturbed individuals – so they believe that we condone their justifications of doing what they do as 'white' supremacist.

The faces of 'hate crimes' are written or spoken of as multicolored or 'multiracial.' That is, when one first hears of a 'hate crime' the first image we generally think of or read is a 'black' victim and a 'white' aggressor. Or even, a 'white' victim and a 'black' aggressor. I'm aware that these so-called groups just happen to be the groups who have a storied history of violence upon another. Yet, the continued high profile of primarily 'black' and 'white' only perpetuate the American belief in 'races.'

A more recent case in point is a September 26, 1999 front-page treatment on 'hate crime' in New York Times Magazine. The author, Andrew Sullivan, begins with the celebrated 'hate crime' in Texas that I noted above. As with all articles of 'hate crime,' before the first paragraph ends, we know the 'race' of the participants involved. Yet, Sullivan goes on to make some very key points. He asks, "Why is hate for a group worse than hate for a person? In Laramie, Wyo., the now-famous epicenter of 'homophobia' where Matthew Shepard was beaten to death; in the months preceding, a 15-year-old pregnant girl was found east of town stabbed 17 times and left for dead. In 1998, an 8-year-old girl was abducted, raped, and murdered by a pedophile, who disposed her body in a garbage dump. Neither, was these killings were was deemed a 'hate crime.' 5

Further, Sullivan states: "Which crime was more frightening this summer [of 1999] the mentally ill Buford

Furrow's [an avowed 'racist' – remember my chapter 'Racist are Mentally Ill] – crazed attacks in Los Angeles, killing one, or Mark Barton murdering his family and several random day-traders in Atlanta, killing 12? Almost certainly the latter. But only Furrow was guilty of a 'hate.'"

Also, Sullivan notes that 'hate crime' advocates counter that extra penalties should be imposed on 'hate crimes' because there is an "epidemic" of such crimes. I suggest that if there is an 'epidemic' of such crimes, it primarily indicates that there is an 'epidemic of CRIME and more Americans with inclinations to commit crimes. We would be better off focusing on why this is occurring among all Americans today and historically, without using 'race' or 'otherness' or 'hate' as an excuse.

Sullivan concludes that, "The truth is, the distinction between a crime filled with personal hate and a crime filled with group hate is an essentially arbitrary one" (Much like, as I've stated earlier, distinctions of 'race' and 'color.') "It tells us nothing interesting about the psychological contours of the specific actor or the specific victim. It [a hate crime] is a function primarily of politics, of special interest groups carving out particular protections for themselves, rather than a serious response to serious criminal concern.

"In an attempt to repudiate a past that treated people differently because of the color of their skin, their sex, or religion, or sexual orientation, <u>we may merely create a future that permanently treats people differently because of their color, sex, religion or sexual orientation</u>. This notion of a hate crime, and the concept of hate behind it, takes a psychological mystery and turns it into a facile political artifact. Rather than compounding this error . . . we should seriously consider repealing the concept altogether."

In conclusion, when we don't challenge or teach young people to challenge the irrational logic of 'hate crimes' and expose them for what they really are – the remnants and guilt from the legacy of racism – then all Americans will continue to fall victim to a perpetuation of 'race-based' and 'minority-based' legislation. 'Hate crimes' and 'affirmative action'- type legislation based in 'race' or 'color' or 'minority' language will only divide us more as 'races' and 'others', instead of bringing us together as Americans.

1-Jacobs, James and Potter, Kimberly, "Hate Crimes – Criminal Law and Identity Politics"

2- Los Angeles Times, May 5, 1999, "Hate Crimes Rose 15% in L.A. County Schools

3- Richard Dooling, New York Times Book Review.

4- Los Angeles Times, August 26, 1999.

5- "The Fight Against Hate" – Andrew Sullivan, New York Times Magazine

Chapter 7 The Pitfalls of Using 'Race' in the American Discourse

"The notion of 'race' is so charged with emotional force that objective discussion of its significance is uncommonly difficult."

— Juan Comas, "Racial Myths"

A situation in which a desired outcome or solution is impossible to attain because of a set of inherently illogical rules or conditions.

- Definition for Catch-22 –American Heritage Dictionary

The American Heritage Dictionary's initial definition for Catch-22 above could also be a good definition for how the various words and concepts of 'race' work within American society. 'Race' consistently creates situations were rational solutions are impossible to attain because of the illogical rules an conditions inherent in the concept of 'race.'

The various words and concepts of 'race' have historically and continue to be land mines for misrepresentations, confusion and divisiveness in America. Cornel West notes that, "Racial' reasoning conceals presuppositions of 'race' behind a deceptive cloak of 'racial' consensus – yet 'racial' reasoning is seductive because it invokes an undeniable history of 'racial' abuse and 'racial' struggle." 1 This is indeed one of the paradoxes of racism's legacy. Dependent as it is on concepts of 'race' and 'color,' all Americans including African-Americans feel compelled to honor the irrationality of its logic because American history has, for example only documented abuse toward 'blacks' or 'Negroes' and not Americans of African ancestry.

Similarly, David Lionel Smith notes that our common sense racial notions subvert our ability to produce accurate accounts of our social circumstances. 2 *I like to paraphrase Smith's important observation as follows: The seductive and seemingly common sense notions of 'race' 'color' and 'minority' status undermine our ability to produce accurate accounts of our social relationships, social conflicts and social identities.*

Thus, historically and to the present, American leaders with a fraction of African ancestry and obvious European ancestry, have claimed to be of the 'black race' and thus 'black' leaders.   Leaders such as Colin Powell, Julian Bond, Danny Bakewell of Los Angeles presently and in the past Frederick Douglass, W.E.B. DuBois, Rev. Dr. Martin Luther King, Jr.,   A. Philip Randolph, Booker T. Washington and Malcolm X all had immediate – parent or grandparent – European ancestry. Yet, they all claimed to be only 'black' or 'Negro.'

After making such claims and after having society repeated tell you that you are in fact 'racialized' then it is only inevitable that humans accept these labels as natural. Yet, when we are talking about well-educated leaders of people who personally know of their European-American parent or grandparent, one can readily see the power of internalizing the 'race' concept.

It is not known if he claimed to be a 'Negro' or 'black' but Patrick Francis Healy has the distinction of having the tallest building at Georgetown University in Washington, D.C. named after him. In 1998, on my first visit to the school, I approached the majestic building in awe. It is a stunning example of 19th century architecture of which I'm a fan. Upon reaching the base of the building I read the inscription of the man of which it is named for and was amazed to discover that Healy was the first 'black' President of a major university. As an African-American, I was first filled with pride to now know this – in the 41st year of my life no less – then immediately became angry. Granted, it is nice to know that Mr. Healy had recent African ancestry – later I found that his mother was a 'mulatto' slave, half African and half European, and his father was an Irish planter.3   His brother in fact, James Augustine, ordained a priest in Paris, France, later became the first 'black' bishop in the U.S. in Portland, Maine. But the question at hand here is: did either of the Healy brothers consider themselves 'black'?   In fact, the picture of Patrick Francis at Georgetown showed him to be of low melanin skin pigmentation and straight hair!

Another case in point was Walter White, NAACP President from 1931 to 1955. In "Who is Black" F. James

Davis notes that Mr. White was estimated to have only 1/64th African ancestry, yet, "he had fair skin, fair hair and blue eyes. When he told whites that he was black, they would often say, 'Are you sure?' He chose not to pass as white." Davis also adds that Rev. Dr. Martin Luther King Jr. had an Irish grandmother and some American Indian ancestry."

American adults today who were of teenage or adult age in the mid-1960s or anyone who has studied American history of the '60s know that the Civil Rights Act was a struggle for the rights of African-Americans, or known then as 'Negroes' 'colored' or 'black' people. In fact, David Twomey notes that, "The legislative history of Title VII of the Civil Rights Act demonstrates that a primary purpose of the act is to provide fair employment opportunities for black Americans. The terms *race* and *color* (emphasis his) as used in the act clearly apply to blacks, and thus the protections of the act are applied to blacks based on race and color." 4 Here is an important example of how the continued use of 'race' and 'color' act to perpetuate the stigma of 'otherness' toward those Americans already victimized by 'racial' classifications. Yet, there is another, paradoxical pitfall that results from using the 'language of racism' in American legislation, demonstrates a key pitfall when using 'race' in the American discourse.

Twomey continues, "However, [since] the word *race was* used, in the act applies to all . . . whites are also protected against discrimination because of [their] race and color. For example, two white professors at a predominately black university were successful in discrimination suits against the university where it was held that the university discriminated against them based on race and color in tenure decisions – Turgeon v. Howard University, 32 FEP 927 (D.C. DC 1983). Yes, the concept of 'reverse discrimination' is a direct result and pitfall of 'racial' reasoning and its inclusion in the American discourse. Because 'race' is an accepted human reality by most Americans, including American lawmakers, it can be rationally found that there is a 'legal construction of 'race' 5 in the United States.

Claims of 'reverse discrimination' – despite the fact of being based on the false logic of 'race' – do nothing toward improving human relations among Americans. In fact, it produces a major pitfall: a perpetuation of false ideas of 'race' and an increased polarization that leads to an unnecessary increase in hostilities among fellow Americans.

As Juan Comas stated at the top of this chapter, the mere mention of 'race' – like the so-called 'race card' – trumps any possibility for objective and constructive discussions on our social relation problems. The proposed and so-called "Dialogue on Race" initiated by President Clinton was just recent evidence that this is true. It is important as educators and parents that we recognize the 'cognitive defects' that the concepts of 'race' create for us in our thought patterns.

The conclusions that we must all, at some point, come to is that the elimination of our concepts of 'race' 'color' and 'minority' status and the use of a BOLD AMERICAN OUTLOOK among American young people is the most logical solution to the pitfalls of using 'race' in the American discourse.

1- West, Cornel – "Race Matters" – 1993.

2- Smith, David Lionel – "What is Black Culture" 1997.

3- Davis, James – "Who is Black" – 1991.

4- Twomey, David P. – "Equal Employment Opportunity Law" - 1990.

5- Haney-Lopez, Ian – "White by Law: The Legal Construction of Race" – 1996.

Chapter 8 Recognizing Racism as a Historical Construct

"Race is indeed a sociohistorical concept."
  – Howard Winant and Michael Omi.1

As responsible educators and parents, teaching a BOLD AMERICAN OUTLOOK to young people we MUST emphasize that today racism is a historical construct and that the term should always be used in the past tense as a legacy that is being perpetuated, which, in fact, is the case. I, for instance, suggest that when the historical fact that IS racism is used in the American discourse, it should be called: racism's legacy.

Unfortunately today, the mode and manner by which the discourse on racism's legacy transpires, we often mention racism as a present-day phenomenon that just IS. Nothing could be further from the truth. The BOLD AMERICAN OUTLOOK must teach and show young people that racism's legacy is not only history based, but also an 'historical construct.' Meaning that racism is based in a historical view, and an old-world view of human identity and reality. Moreover, we must teach young people that racism's legacy is representative of a bygone era that will chain them unnecessarily. This does not mean that they should ignore racism's legacy. They should though, think of racism' legacy an historical marker in human history and an era that we must never return to, let alone repeat as we often do when we use the 'language of racism.'

Seeing racism as primarily a historical fact rather than a present-day reality is especially difficult for adults today. Particularly for those who feel that they are still victimized by racism's legacy. These individuals have valid reasons to believe that present-day racism effects their lives. Yet, what they fail to understand is that in the adult world today, at the end of our second millennium, there are just too many adults with power and influence who just refuse to believe or are just not capable of believing that 'racial' and 'color' and 'minority' identities are not human realties. In short, there are just too many Americans who have been infested or have contracted the cancer of racism's legacy.

And, they just accept racism and the concept of race as 'natural' or man-made problems that cannot be remedied.

Yet, the BOLD AMERICAN OUTLOOK contends that many adults today, particularly educators, can prevent America's young people from contracting the cancer of racism's legacy, which continues to live and breathe primarily through the 'language of racism' within American schools. In the same manner, concerned adults must cease using the 'language of racism' by avoiding the various words and concepts of 'race,' 'color' and 'minority' status in their homes.

We should never give our young people any reason to believe or understand that 'racism' is something that just exist, without any ways or means for <u>them</u> to do anything about it when they mature into adults. It is my firm belief that any child that matures with a BOLD AMERICAN OUTLOOK will readily understand how to use the historical nature of racism's legacy as a foundation to build a strong sense of character. This sense of character will be fundamentally strong enough to combat the inevitable onslaught of the historical momentum of racism's legacy with Courage, Fairness and Cultural Respect.

A major aspect of having a BOLD AMERICAN OUTLOOK is to understand the outer dimensions of racism' legacy. That dimension is essentially historical. We adults do not sense racism to be historical because we perceive it through a lens tarnished with the 'language of racism.' Educators and parents must take steps to educate young people to understand this dynamic of racism's legacy: Racism's legacy is a remnant of a bygone era – YOU have the power to either bring an end to that era in your lifetime or bear the consequences of living in the past.

1- Howard Winant and Michael Omi, in "Racial Formation in the United States" 1986

Chapter 9 Proof That 'Race' Does Not Exist

"Race is one of central conceptual inventions of modernity."
– David Theo Goldberg – "Racist Culture" 1993.

"However powerful and however deeply a part of our [American] society race may be, races are still only a human invention.
– Ian F. Haney Lopez – "White by Law"- 1996.

For many educated adults and educators, the fact that 'race' does not exist as a human quality is something they probably would not deny. Yet, access to proof of this by scholars and writers on this subject can be hard to easily find. The purpose of this chapter is to give you as many examples as I can find that 'race' does not exist. This will not only help you further your understanding on this manner, but more importantly, you must provide this information to young people, so that they can use it and apply it to their own conclusions or life experiences.

I shall begin with the words of the man most responsible for helping me forge a greater understanding of the non-reality of what I was told from childhood – that I a member of a 'race' the 'black race.' In "Man's Most Dangerous Myth – The Fallacy of Race" Ashley Montagu, begins Chapter One with, "The idea of "race" represents one of the most dangerous myths of our time, and one of the most tragic. Myths are most dangerous when they remain unrecognized for what they are." This was certainly true for me and I would assume you too. For a little over a decade into my adult life, I believe that 'race' was a true human reality. And thus, I tried to accept my 'otherness' and deal as best I could with the perceptions of my inferiority as another 'race' the generally perceived 'inferior race' in America.

Montagu concludes the first chapter [of the 5th edition] with, "Today, many of us believe in "race." "Race is the witchcraft of our time. The means by which we exorcise our demons. It is the contemporary myth. Man's most dangerous myth." How ironic it is that something written in 1974, over a generation ago, is still pertinent and sadly true today. Likewise, in the Introduction, Montagu relates that " . . . the Joint Commission on Mental Health in Children published in 1970 stated that, "Racism was the number one health problem facing America."1 Has that changed today? Maybe. But we also must admit that we rarely acknowledge the true magnitude of racism's legacy on America's young people today.

In the 6th edition, Montagu states, "the myth of race is not the fact that physically distinguishable populations of humans exist. [This is obvious, but has more do with how our ancestor's genes reacted to their environment]. But rather to the belief that races are populations or peoples whose physical differences are innately linked to with significant differences in mental capacities, and that these innate hierarchical differences are measurable by cultural achievements or standardized intelligence (IQ) test. "2

Montagu continues that, "Richard Lewontin, a professor of genetics at Harvard University, who carried out an important investigation of genetic diversity in the human species concluded that, "It is clear that our perception of relatively large differences between human races [are] indeed a biased perception . .. human populations are remarkably similar to each other. Human racial classifications are of no social value and are positively destructive to social and human relations. Since such racial classification is now seen to be of virtually no genetic or taxonomic significance, no justification can be offered for their continuance." Montagu continues that such facts render the concept of 'race' and the continuance of 'race' classifications erroneous and obsolescent . . . for such reasons, modern biologist find that the use of the concept of 'race' should be discontinued."3

Likewise, David Theo Goldberg relates that the difference between humans is significantly insignificant, "Humans beings possess a far larger proportion of genes in common than they do genes that are supposed to differentiate them racially. Not surprisingly, we are much more like each other than we are different. It has been estimated that the difference in difference – the percentage of our genes that determine our purportedly racial or primarily morphological differences – is 0.5 percent."4

Howard Winant and Michael Omi, in "Racial Formation in the United States" emphatically state that "The social sciences have come to reject biologistic notions of race in favor of an approach which regard race as a social concept." They further state that, "Spurred on by the classification scheme of living organisms divised by Carolus Linnaeus' Systema Naturae, many scholars in the 18th and 19th centuries dedicated themselves to the identification and ranking of variations in humankind. Race was thought of as a biological concept, yet its precise definition was the subjects of debates which continue to rage today. Despite efforts ranging from Dr. Samuel Morton's studies of cranial capacity to contemporary attempts to base racial classification on shared gene pools, the concept of race has defied biological definition."5

In "African-American Acculturation" Hope Landrine and Elizabeth A. Klonoff claim that Psychology is the only social science that continues to use and recognize 'race' as a model for its studies. Here they give the social science of psychology, 'Five Reason to Unmake America's Races':

1.   – *Race is more than a word; rather it is also a theoretical model of difference.* The theoretical mode of difference entailed in the concept of race is harmful to individuals, groups and society; is morally repugnant; lacks empirical evidence and thereby does not advance science; and maintains racial stratification.

2.   *The concept of race racializes European-Americans as well as African-Americans.* Race thereby obstructs psychology's understanding of 'whites' because it ignores the cultural differences among the diversity of cultures defined as the 'white' race.

3.   *The concept of race is unscientific.* Psychology's continuing use of it (despite its rejection by other sciences) renders the discipline ludicrous in

the eyes of other sciences, as well as in the eyes of much of the public.

4.   *As long as the concept of race remains, neither tolerant cultural pluralism in society nor an appreciation diversity in psychology can be achieved*; for these are negated by maintaining a superior, 'white' race.

5.   *As long as the concept of race remains in psychology and (thus) in the public consciousness, powerful persons and groups remain free to use it.* Any of the many cultural groups (e.g., Latinos) in this nation can be defined as races, and will be so defined under specific social and economic conditions. Psychology must reject this concept because psychology alone maintains the concept. The only way to do so is to de-racialize African-Americans (and with them, European-Americans).

Landrine and Klonoff conclude that, "Thus the need to dismantle and destroy race and races is pressing. So long as a "black" and (in particular) a "white" race exist, we do not believe that an appreciation of cultural diversity can be achieved."

MORE PROOF

"Race" is not a physical thing but a cultural artifact . . . Despite the pseudoscience of eugenics, race vanishes at the molecular (genetic) level."
   – Eric Mark Kramer, "Postmodernism and Race" 1997.

"Neither race nor related concepts can be used in any scientifically precise sense to refer to the people inhabiting this planet today, after centuries of genetic intermixtures."
         – Thomas Sowell, "Race and Culture" – 1994

"The term race was first a kind of classification invented by Europeans: First, to press the political claims of groups within European countries. Then, to represent relations between these countries. Only later when potentialities of this way of labeling people had been extended and biological theories integrated with social ones, was it imposed on upon the rest of the world." – Banton and Harwood, "The Race Concept" – 1975.

"The term 'race' was applied to varieties of Homo sapiens in the middle of the 18th century by Buffon, the French naturalist. Prior to this time race was a term used to describe breeds of domestic animals. Since then the term has been used in a variety of social and biological contexts and ahs become encumbered with contradictory and imprecise meanings. Many people take for granted that they know what race means and assume that scientific investigation has long ago proved the existence of significant human racial differences . . . There is even a considerable confusion over the number of divisions of humanity; as few as three and as many as 37 races have been described. What constitutes a race is a hard question to answer, because one's classification usually depends on the purpose . . .." – Stephen Moldar, "Human Variation" – 1983.

There are literally countless other examples of proof that the concept of 'race' is non-existent and thus should be done away with. The April 15th, 1995 edition of the Los Angeles Times ran an excellent article, "Is the Concept of Race a Relic?" by Robert Lee Hotz. Of course the definitive work on the fallacy of 'race' is "Man's Most Dangerous Myth" by Ashley Montagu. More recently, books that claim to deconstruct 'race' and offer 'postmodernist' views on racism's legacy abound, such as, "The Racialization of America" by Yehudi O. Webster and "Critical Race Theory" edited by Kimberle Crenshaw.

It is my sincere wish that you do your own investigation of these works and others to confirm for yourself that the only answer is what I've said all along. We must eliminate the 'language of racism' and we can start by educating America's young people with a BOLD AMERICAN OUTLOOK.

Chapter 10 Stress the Embracing of Culture and NOT 'Race'

"The history of our species tells us that cultural diversity is the creative force in our history."
– John Collier, "The Creative Value of Cultural Diversity" 1946. 1

"*Cultural categories are much more readily accessible as sources of pertinent information.*

– Michael Vannoy Adams 2

The BOLD AMERICAN OUTLOOK emphatically urges educators and parents to teach young people that they must not only learn about other cultures, but we must also embrace and celebrate them as if they were our own. The more each of us knows and celebrates another culture the less likelihood of stereotypes, anxiety or fear of someone of another cultural heritage.

A key point for us to remember is that there is real POWER when people of diverse cultures come together and celebrate the various things that make each unique.

Take for example a food fair or the recent phenomenon of "the Taste of's" – the growing occasion of bringing samples of all the eating establishments in a given city or region. Here you have restaurants that specialize in foods from various cultures and locales –local and international. The foods available for 'tasting' are known, properly, as are the people: French, Italian, Polish, Mexican, Chinese, African/Soul Food, German, Japanese, Jewish or Caribbean foods in addition to traditional American delicacies.

Can you imagine if only American burgers, steaks and traditional American food were all there was to eat, not only at these 'Tastes" but also for all of our meals, just because we live in what we call America. Can you imagine never being able to buy a pizza, taco, egg roll, sushi, polish sausage, soul food or lox and bagel whenever you wanted to. What makes these 'Tastes' so wonderful is not just the food, but the great diversity of the foods.

This to is what makes our world so wonderful - The great diversity of humans. There are so many interesting things about each of us that make life such a wonderful journey. And one of the most interesting things about life is learning about the differences in human life. I'm certain that if we spent more of our time asking questions about another person's cultural heritage, each of us would discover and find so much more to talk about and share with one another. We will also discover more about ourselves and how much we have in common with others – who we thought were completely different – because they to are, more likely than not, American too.

In addition, asking others about their cultural heritage would reduce the possibilities for fear and anxiety about others. Here is where a primary BOLD AMERICAN OUTLOOK principle – COURAGE – comes into play. Ridding ourselves of our fears of others is also such a wonderful feeling. It's like taking a heavy load off your back and gaining a new outlook – a BOLD AMERICAN OUTLOOK.

Why Stress Culture

Because the experiences that are stored and passed down within the cultures of our parents and ancestors are what make each individual and us what they are today. The totality of those cultural experiences within the United States can make this nation much more productive and harmonious than it is today. Yet, presently, a large part of those experiences are ignored or denied expression because they are cloaked under a shroud of 'race' 'color' and 'minority' terms.

Cultural identity and expressions are the lifeblood of a people or society. As the "Taste of" analogy above demonstrates, it is when humans express their cultural uniqueness and then share it with others who are not of their cultural heritage is when the fullness of life is actually expressed.

There are many reasons for the educator/parent to stress the cultural identities and integrity of a student/child and the culture they identify with. There are many books that stress the importance of the awareness of students/children's cultural identity for educators and parents. Instead of attempting to detail the many key points here, I strongly suggest that any educator or parent, concerned about the confusing nature of identity and identity politics should read the following:

"Multicultural Counseling in Schools" by Paul Pedersen and John C. Carey

"Increasing Multicultural Understanding" by Don C. Locke

"African-American Acculturation" by Hope Landrine and Elizabeth Klonoff

"Who is Black" by F. James Davis

"Multicultural Counseling Competencies by Derald Wing Sue et al., *Sage*

Now a word of caution. Some, if not all, of these books do use the various words and concepts within the 'language of racism' and this is due to as stated in the "Logical Conclusion" that many writers and scholars on human relations, past and present, have not taken the logical conclusion that the BOLD AMERICAN OUTLOOK takes, i.e., the suppression of the very terms that work to reify or perpetuate the very problems that they report. For a detailed account of how this phenomenon works, please read, "The Racialization of America" by Yehudi O. Webster.

1-Collier, John – from "Man's Most Dangerous Myth" – A. Montagu.

2-Adams, Michael Vannoy, "The Multicultural Imagination" 1996

Chapter 11 We Must Accept A 'Generational Discourse Gap'

"The power of the media lies not only in their ability to reflect the dominant 'racial' ideology, but also their capacity to shape that ideology initially to the public."
-Michael Omi and Howard Winant, "Racial Formation in the U.S."

As educator/parents and as teachers of the BOLD AMERICAN OUTLOOK, we must accept and welcome a 'Generational Discourse Gap' in regard to ending racism's legacy with America's young people because it is not only necessary, it is inevitable. Look at the example of Tiger Woods.

Mr. Woods is an American of obvious diverse cultural ancestry to most adults. When he burst upon the scene a few years ago, becoming the youngest person to ever win the Masters Golf Championship, an issue began over what IS he. Is he 'black'? Is he 'brown'? Is he Asian? Is he Cambodian? Just what are you Tiger? - Was a constant question at press interviews.

Tiger finally set everyone straight by proclaiming, "Growing up, I came up with this name: I'm a Cablinasian." Ca-bl-in-asian. 'Ca' for his Caucasian ancestry. 'Bl' for his 'black' ancestry. 'In for his Native American Indian ancestry and 'Asian' for his Cambodian ancestry.

Of course, if I were there I would have praised him for defining himself and not letting others define him, but also inform him that he does not have 'black' ancestry, but rather, African or African-American ancestry. I also would question if his Caucasian roots really go back to the Caucasus Mountains near Mt. Ararat?

Yet the greater message here is this: some of the more enlightened and BOLD among us, such as Mr. Woods, are already beginning to forge – though perhaps unawares – a BOLD AMERICAN OUTLOOK to other Americans who are still trapped in the old-world view of humans as 'races' as 'colored' or a 'minority.'

The danger that these categories and classifications do is that they lump and label individuals into convenient niches that most of us would not like have done to ourselves. The reality is that for the great majority of Americans, our personal ancestry is just as complex if not more so as Tiger Wood's ancestry is. We should, as he does, recognize and share all these ancestries with everyone or all that inquire.

Why am I not a 'White' Guy

My own ancestry includes French, Irish, African and Native American. Yet looking at me, you might just assume that I'm just a 'black' guy with ONLY African ancestry. This is a common mistake made toward millions of Americans that look like me. In fact, if I were to accept the absurd logic known as 'hypo-descent'1 that has made so many Americans that look like me ONLY 'black' despite my varied ancestry, I could just as well call myself 'white.'

Because the so-called logic of hypo-descent or 'the one-drop rule' claims that any part of one's parentage or ancestry makes you only one 'race,' yet, usually the perceived subordinate 'race.' Thus, because of the arbitrary nature of 'race' assignment. I could claim to be 'white' or even the equally inaccurate and false identity – 'Indian.'

Yet, since I do not believe in the false logic of hypo-descent – which also furthers the false concept of 'blood transmission' during procreation2 – I certainly do not consider myself to be 'white' though technically I could using this so-called logic that tragically is still in use today. The tragedy herein is that when the cross-cultural phenotype of one's parent or grandparents' is obviously evident, then the child, historically and to present-day, grows up being told by society that he/she is ONLY one or the other 'race' or even a 'mixed race' or 'biracial' person.

This sort of labeling is entirely unnecessary. 'Race' labels only help toward perpetuating the false concepts of 'races' and add nothing toward helping individuals understand the reality of their true diverse cultural heritages and our commonality as Americans.

In the end here, I must make a plea to all adult Americans and educators who wish to help young people end racism' legacy with a BOLD AMERICAN OUTLOOK. We must be tolerant and accept a 'Generational Discourse Gap' – the possibility of wide variety of claims of diverse cultural heritages or inventive titles from American young people, such as "Cablinasian" that Tiger Woods came up with. This is the necessary process that all young people need to go through to recognize and understand their own culturally diverse ancestry and just as importantly, to understand and appreciate the diversity of others.

1. F. James Davis, "Who is Black" - 1991
2. Ashley Montagu, "Man's Most Dangerous Myth"- 1964

Chapter 12 Biggest Resistors To Changing 'Color' Identifiers

" . . . Tolerance of absurdities, lurk in the best of minds. "
— Yehudi O. Webster.

The 'color' coding of individuals and groups is so entrenched within the 'language of racism' that one can correctly say that 'colored' people – 'black' 'white' – are traditional American identifiers of humans for 'race' and difference reasons. Americans and particularly such American institutions as government and educational institutions, medical institutions and the media – frequently use 'white' to identify persons of low-melanin and European phenotype and 'black' to identify persons of high-melanin and African phenotype. We have discussed all of the discursive reasons why these vague and inaccurate terms can and have caused problems in the United States.

One reason that is rarely spoken on though is that a great majority of Americans seem content with their 'color' label and even resist efforts or suggestions to change. The BOLD AMERICAN OUTLOOK has the view that those who are resistant to change from terms that perpetuate 'racial' categories and the racism that is a result, are basically ignorant to the fact that this is so. Another is the power of language to actually shape thought and action. In "Language and Prejudice Toward Negroes" Simon Podair noted that " So powerful is the role of language in its imprint upon the human mind that even the ethnic group may begin to accept the very expression that aid in its stereotyping." We clearly see that this is evident today among African-Americans today who, from personal observations, consistently use 'black' 'Negro' and the 'N-word' among themselves. On the use of the term 'black' Podair concludes, "Again, even the [culture] group whose interest run counter to the symbolic use of this word in our culture may accept it as a part of its own language patterns.1

With all the historical baggage and symbolic violence2 that come with terms of 'color' and the discursive negative images that they convey, one would think that the culture group that would most want to erase America's 'color' projections would be African-Americans. The color 'black' is, after all, perhaps the most negative word in the English language. The word also has a natural negative association. For instance, the term Thanatos3, a universal or natural human fear of darkness or 'blackness' has some merit to it – more on this later.

My personal experience with has shown that so-called 'blacks' are much more resistant to change than so-called 'whites.' The great majority of European-American adults do not seem to have any basic obsession with 'whiteness' with the exception being so-called 'white' supremacist and those in American institutions and the media who consistently write statistics showing the difference between 'whites and blacks'. While the great majority of African-American adults that I've spoken to <u>are</u> obsessed with their 'blackness' primarily because they've grown to look at 'blackness' as a symbol of pride, reminiscent of the old James Brown song, "Say It Loud, I'm Black and I'm Proud."

Of European-Americans the overwhelming group that fosters a belief in 'whiteness' are so-called 'white' supremacist. In her book "White Man Falling – Race, Gender and White Supremacy" Abby Ferber explains "White supremacist discourse is strange to read for many reasons, but one of the most obvious is its overt focus on whiteness." Thus, eliminating the concept of 'whiteness' by showing the falseness of the term would be beneficial in regard to defusing a key element within these so-called 'white' groups alone. It will also show just how off-base they are in regard to there own self-identity and how ignorant they are of their true cultural identity.

While the difficulty with so-called 'whites' is basically institutional with the exception of the extremist 'white' supremacist, African-Americans in general, across a wide spectrum take their 'blackness' personally and thus have internalized this 'color' consciousness within their various social institutions.

And here is were the greatest resistance toward changing 'color' may well occur. Most African-Americans are comfortable with such titles as: the NAACP – the "National Association of for the Advancement of Colored People"; "The United Negro College Fund" that now tries to pass itself off as simply UNCF (who just received a $1billion grant from Bill Gates as long as the money goes to so-called Negroes); BET – the "Black Entertainment Network"; "Black Enterprise" magazine and the TV show "America's Black Forum." Various other African-American institutions such as those associated with various lawyer groups, medical groups, media groups, law enforcement groups and church groups that all use "black' to define their cause or affiliation with 'blackness." Surprisingly, with the exception of 'white' supremacist groups, there are few similar groups with predominant European-American members that are defined or named as explicitly 'White' groups to show their 'white' affiliations and one can imagine that if there were, there would be an outcry over their use of the term 'white' in their title.

The intent here is not to denigrate so-called 'black' groups and associations. As an American of African ancestry myself I can sympathize and empathize with the purpose and need of such groups. Yet, what I must emphasize here again is that we must teach our young people to go beyond affiliations with groups with such titles because, quite honestly, they are a direct result of racism's legacy. They evolved as a result of systematic and institutional exclusions within American government, economic and political organizations.

The purpose of a BOLD AMERICAN OUTLOOK is to educate young people to recognize that these exclusions existed historically, but that does not mean that they must exist when they reach adulthood. In fact, though many of the so-called 'black' groups are still active, the goal should be to change their titles to state their African-American cultural status and to encourage other Americans to join or attend since they too are American.

We have to teach our young people that any American should feel comfortable and welcome to any other organization that includes a cultural and American reference in their title. Thus, any American should be welcomed and feel welcomed to any Jewish-American organization, and likewise any Latino-American should be welcomed to an African-American organization and any European-American welcomed to an Asian-American organization etc. Such affiliations across cultural boundaries with a recognition that we are all Americans is something that we MUST teach our young people to strive for as we move and as they mature into the 21st century.

I must clarify here that that the great majority of resistors to changing 'color' titles will not be young people, or at least not the very young people, most will be adults like you and I, who have been raised and socialized to believe that 'races' and 'colored' people. Also, and unfortunately, it will be those adults who most likely identify with being called 'black' or 'white.'

Some or even many young people of high school age will be resistant for sure. But it is my sincere hope that most young people at this age will be familiar with the BOLD AMERICAN OUTLOOK before they reach high school age, but of course, we cannot simply write-off high school age young people, thus, educators and parents, please feel free to introduce the BOLD AMERICAN OUTLOOK to high school age young people if you sincerely believe that it can have a positive effect on their lives or education.

1 – Simon Podair, in "White Racism" – Barry Schwartz and Robert Disch, 1972.

2 – Karen A. Callaghan, 'Symbolic Violence and Race' in "Postmodernism and Race"

3 – Robert Bosnak, pp22 in "The Multicultural Imagination" – Michael Vannoy Adams.

4 – Abby L. Ferber, "White Man Falling" - 1998

Chapter 13 A Self-proclaimed 'Racist' Is Actually Mentally Ill

"Racism is a mental illness characterized by perceptual distortion, a denial of reality, delusions of grandeur (belief in 'white' supremacy), the projection of blame (on the victim), and phobic reactions to differences . . .
— *Gerald Pine and Asa Hillard.* 1

"There is no health in a society afflicted by racism — Thurgood Marshall
from — "Racism and Mental Health" 1973

There are no true 'racist.' The only true 'racist' were those who lived long ago. They sincerely believed that they and others were 'races' due to limited information they had about other cultural groups. In addition, the prejudiced reasoning of 18th Century biologist and social scientist comforted the layman's uneducated views.2 Thus; social systems of exclusion and inclusion began in early America to mirror their beliefs. Those who claim to be 'racist' today are not really true 'racist,' more accurately they are perpetuators of an old-world view of 'race' and ignorance of the cultural essence of all humans. When we look at the term 'racist.' We now know that all the various words associated with 'race' are invalid, false and empty. Moreover, to call or accuse a person of being 'racist' is an empty claim and unintentionally reaffirms their belief that 'race' is a reality. Put simply, though 'racist' had some validity centuries ago, today and since, all the term really does is legitimizes an archaic concept to the present-day.

Since 'racist' has no real meaning, what is a person who is a self-proclaimed 'racist'?

The answer is mentally ill. Any person that knowingly believes that humans are indeed 'races' and thus subject to the old-world views of superiority and inferiority, in addition to an absence of a true culture, is indeed mentally unstable. This is especially the case when you consider all the recent and current information that rejects any idea of 'races.'

And, there is much evidence that prove why self-proclaimed 'racists' are mentally unstable. Perhaps predominant is acute insecurity and a obsessive need to affiliate or identify with something that he/she believes will give them a sense of power – i.e., 'White' power or 'Black' power, etc.

In "Man's Most Dangerous Myth" Ashley Montagu identified two key psychological concepts that lend evidence to the mental instability of so-called 'racist.': Displacement and Projection.

DISPLACEMENT

The act of displacement is a process whereby an individual displaces aggression from one object to another.

"A considerable amount of the aggressiveness that adults exhibit is originally produced during childhood by parents, teachers, nurses, or whoever else participates in the process of socializing the child. By depriving the infant and later the child of the many means of satisfaction which it seeks . . . expected satisfactions are thwarted and frustration after frustration are piled up within the child. Such frustrations lead to resentment, to fear, to insecurity, to hostility, and to aggressiveness. In childhood, this resentment or aggressiveness is displayed in with a 'bad temper' and in general 'naughtiness.' At this stage of development the child finds himself in a state of severe conflict. He must either control the expression of his aggressiveness or else suffer the punishment and loss of love which his aggressiveness provokes. Such conflicts are usually resolved by excluding the painful situation for consciousness by the repression of one's aggressive energies. These are rarely completely repressed . . . ."

Montagu further explains that, "When the release of aggression toward certain objects or agents is socially interdicted or otherwise made difficult . . . aggressiveness may then be displaced toward some more accessible target. The government, blacks, Jews, Catholics, and foreigners and the like, will conveniently serve as targets, and where such displacement of aggression occurs the object of it becomes the scapegoat. Collective displacement of this sort is a well-known phenomenon . . . Humans in search of a target readily utilize social tension for the displacement of personal tension."

The conclusion here is clear. Aggression in humans is universal. Yet, the expression of one's aggression is dependent on what is socially acceptable within certain social environments. It is no mystery among adults who have a firm knowledge of American history that 'racial' aggression and 'racial' prejudice were prime examples of displacement because, particularly in Southern states, it was socially acceptable to do so. The various members of African-Americans, Native Americans and Asian-Americans culture groups were viewed as 'races' 'colors' and 'minority' people and thus helped to facilitate rationalized acts of aggression and violence.

PROJECTION

Projection the process of attributing to others feelings and impulses originating in ourselves which have been refused conscious recognition.

The psychological aspect of projection are evident all around us since we do, as a people and as nation subscribe to the notions that 'races' and 'colored' people are an adequate means of human identity. In "The Multicultural Imagination" Michael Vannoy Adams states, "Natural 'racial' categories are so vague and elusive that virtually the only purpose they serve is an utterly trivial and inconsequential one – an opportunity for prejudicial projections." Later, he cites that sociologist, Michael Rustin, "considers racism a psychological formation, a very deep structure indeed – an unconscious projection. . . This is paradoxically the source of racism's power. It is the fact that this category means nothing in itself that makes it able to bear so much meaning – mostly psychologically primitive in character – with so little innate resistance from the conscious mind." 4

Here is the answer, perhaps, to why there is indeed so little complaint or even out-and-out rejection of the concepts and classifications of 'race' and 'color' within the American discourse. Particularly by those who are negatively and symbolically affected by 'racial' projections the most, so-called 'blacks.'

Adams further relates that, "It is the low informational value of categories like color that enables racist to endow it with such high projective value. The relative poverty of color allows it to be used – and abused – by racists who empower it with a wealth of significance and project it uncritically. Later Adams tells us that, "Rustin approaches the topic of 'race' semiotically. He notes that 'race' as such, is an empty signifier. [Yet,] Adams claims that, "'Race' has many meaning, which have been projected, both consciously and unconsciously, onto the other. Projection is, of course, a variety of reference . . . When 'race' has been projected onto the other, that other has been referred to as a 'race.'" However, Rustin counters that, "Race is a signifier with no basis in scientific fact, no rational foundation."

The unfortunate reality of all this is that, for the self-proclaimed 'racist,' all of this does not really matter. To the self-proclaimed 'racist' 'race' and 'color' and 'minority' and various other titles they create for humans are indeed human realities. This only gives evidence to the real mental instability of these so-called 'racist' due to their belief in delusions of so-called 'races' and 'colored' people.

Finally, consider this from the preface of "Racism and Mental Health" were the authors together agree that, "Racism is a pathology with personal and social consequences and therefore must be dealt with on the individual as well as the group level."[5]

1 – Asa Hilliard III and Gerald Pine, "Rx for Racism" in Phi Delta Kappan 71 April 1990.

2 – Ashley Montagu, "Man's Most Dangerous Myth: The Fallacy of Race"

3 – Ibid., p. 227

4 – Adams, Michael Vannoy, "The Multicultural Imagination" 1996.

5 – Willie, Charles, "Racism and Mental Health"—1973.

Chapter 14 Ethnicity is NOT 'Race' Ethnicity IS Culture

One of the unfortunate by-products of racism's legacy is that the terms 'ethnicity' or 'ethnic groups' have, in the American public discourse, close associations with images within the 'language of racism.' The BOLD AMERICAN OUTLOOK furthers the view that ethnicity has nothing to do with 'race' 'color' or 'minority' status and that ethnicity is, in fact, culture. With this in mind, the BOLD AMERICAN OUTLOOK strongly suggests that educators and parents stress the use of the word culture over ethnicity or ethnic group when identifying American individuals or human population groups.

Granted the difference between ethnicity and cultures appears insignificant, yet when one considers the reality today is that when many Americans think ethnicity they visualize 'race' and 'color' then one can understand that for many Americans the difference between the two can be significant. This is why we must stress CULTURE over ethnicity because most Americans understand that culture transcends what they understand to be 'race.'

"Cultural categories are much more readily accessible as sources of pertinent information [about humans]," states Michael Vannoy Adams in his book "The Multicultural Imagination." "The reason natural categories like 'color' are so useless (except for racist, for whom they are all too useful) is that they convey very little, if any, information about significant psychical differences."1

Here is a graphic reason why we must avoid ethnicity. With its symbolic associations with 'races' or 'color,' ethnicity has what Adams later refers to as "low informational value" something rarely if ever associated with culture.

Let me be clear here that I do not underestimate the meaning and value of ethnicity. The facts are that there are many ethnic groups amid what we commonly call 'race' and 'color' today. Among so-called 'whites' there are all of the many and varied European-American ethnic groups that are too often lost amid the title of 'whites.'

Among the so-called 'blacks' there are many ethnic groups as well – African-American, Puerto Rican-Americans, Cuban-Americans, Brazilian-Americans, Caribbean-Americans and Canadian-Americans among many more including native Africans who have immigrated and are now naturalized citizens of the United States. But many Americans view 'blacks' as an ethnic group within itself, but nothing could be further from the truth and this is why we must avoid ethnicity.

Among the so-called 'Hispanic race' there are many ethnic groups as well, including some included in the so-called 'black race.' Mexican-Americans, native Central Americans and South Americans and more (see Appendix A – Just Who Are Americans).

The same is true for the so-called 'Asian race' and 'Indian race.' Yet, what we should take from our knowledge of the 'ethnic groups' within these so-called races is that they are more understandable as cultures. Within our man-made 'races' are a great variety of cultures that have – as 'ethnic people' – been disassociated away from 'whites' or European-Americans and thought of only as 'ethnic groups' or 'others' Americans.

Ethnicity is a valid term and mode of describing the differences between human population groups. Unfortunately though, ethnicity again – because of its associations with what we Americans believe is 'race' – has gathered connotations that are too closely aligned with the 'language of racism.' Or put simply, when the faces of 'ethnic groups' are evoked, rarely do images of European-American ethnic groups come to mind.

Ethnicity transcends what we know as 'race' but more importantly CULTURE transcends ethnicity and gets us all on the right page and right path toward solutions to our American dilemma – recognizing our intertwining differences and legacies as culture groups and our commonality as Americans within the borders of these United States.

87

1- Adams, Michael Vannoy, "The Multicultural Imagination" – 1996

Chapter 15 Asking About Identity and Avoiding Identity Crises

*" . . . giving precedence to culture [identity] over biology
. . . calls for a conception of difference that recognizes the
complex and multiple interrelationships among social
structures, the structures and workings of cultural
discourses. . . "*

– Robert G. Dunn 1

Have you ever been in a situation or circumstance where you met or knew of someone on a casual basis, but were not sure of their ancestral identity or nationality? Did you feel awkward about asking them? Did you feel that you might offend them by asking? Have you ever asked a person – What Are You? And then felt embarrassment by the reaction the person gave you.

All of the questions can pose some discomforting situations and the last can be taken as being downright rude. So what is the proper thing to ask? What should you teach your students/children to ask if they're unsure of another's identity?

As you may know by now, the BOLD AMERICAN OUTLOOK teaches that cultural identity and respect are key aspects for young people to understand and nurture as they mature into adulthood. With that in mind, it is important for us adults to begin to help young people to properly identify someone else's CULTURAL identity and how to inquire about it if need be.

We adults must ingrain in our young people's mind a two-fold cultural question. That question should be this: What's your cultural heritage? Or, What's your cultural ancestry? Either of these questions should give any young person (or any adult for that matter) all the initial information that they will need about that person's identity.

Also a key point to remember, as discussed in previously, that the various words and concepts within the 'language of racism' – words convey another's 'race' 'color' or 'minority' status have what is known as "low informational value." This is one of the key facts to remember when teaching young people why they must reject or avoid using the 'language of racism.' The very fact that 'race' 'color' and 'minority' identities give 'low information' about another person's identity is reason enough to avoid using the 'language of racism.'

Alternatively, CULTURAL ancestry and heritage identifiers have "high informational value." Knowledge of another's cultural heritage or ancestry is not only valuable information to have, but it opens up so many opportunities for topics of discussion and discovery.

One of the most unfortunate aspects of our current American discourse with its pervasive obsession with 'race' and 'color' identity is that it does not allow and in many cases even prevents a great majority of Americans from discovering the great variety of complex or dual cultural ancestries among Americans. We are so conditioned to think of one another as just one fixed 'race' or even cultural heritage that we ignore or avoid asking others about their cultural heritage.

Another key point to remember is that one should not ask or inquire about another's nationality because, though of some informational value, an individual can still possess a variety of cultural heritages within a single national identity. For instance, an African-American and European-American are indeed Americans, but their commonality as just Americans tells us little about the individual, their ancestry and even their life experiences though class may well be the most defining in that case.

An important point also to remember is that if a person gives only a national identity, we MUST honor and use THAT identity if that individual desires the use of that identity only. <u>It is incumbent upon the well-informed educator or parent/adult to glean from an uninformed student/child what their true cultural heritage is.</u> This is crucial so that you know, as part of the 'high information' you need to know about that child (unless, of course, you are the biological parent of that child). Also, and perhaps more importantly, the child will then know their cultural heritage, so that he/she can begin to recognize the rich cultural value within their cultural ancestry. **<u>This is a very key self-esteem component that is lacking in young people who claim to be only 'white' or 'black.'</u>** Many educators have complained in the past and present of their distress over what they see as developmental disorders that are a result of a lack of awareness, by the young person, of their true cultural identity. 2

Human Identity is Either Dual or Complex

Likewise, some young people like to claim that they are simply American. This is usually the response from a child who is unaware of the cultural ancestry of their parents or are of recent multicultural ancestry (or what we call today 'mixed race' or 'biracial') and choose to avoid any confusion or controversy over their ancestral identity. For instance, some young people in the latter category feel that they will ignore one parent or the other by choosing to be just 'black' or 'white' or even African-American or European-American if their parents identify with one or the other identity.

Here is a good opportunity to show the young person that they are not just American or one 'race' or 'color.' Also, you can show the young person the benefit of revealing their cultural identity because cultural identity MUST be either dual or complex. This must be stressed to young people and here is how.

First, the student/child is most likely an American, so always affirm that he/she is correct there. But also inform them that their parent(s) or perhaps grandparent/great-grandparent or beyond, identifies with another culture or nation and that it is very important that the student/child also identify with that culture so that they can carry forth the traditions of that culture if they should have children. Further explain, particularly to older young people that cultures are very important to the human experience and human history which is why they must know or discover their own cultural heritage.

You have now have helped confirm to the young person that their identity is at least dual: their American identity and the identity of their parent(s) if their parent(s) claim a single cultural identity such as Chinese, Italian, French, Mexican, Sioux, or African. Thus, the student/child can now claim to that his/her identity is: Chinese-American;

Italian-American; French-American, Mexican-American, Native Sioux-American; or African-American.

But what if the student/child or the educator/parent knows that the child's recent ancestry is more than one culture. Here is where the complexity of humanity and each individual become evident. As noted in Chapter 10, Tiger Woods is a recent high-profile example of an American who refuses to be placed in a single 'racial' category and who seeks to inform all of his complex cultural ancestry. He even came up with his own name for it "Cablinasian" to inform others his various cultural heritages. <u>THIS is of 'high informational value' because it tells others that Mr. Woods is not just 'black' or even just African-American.</u> He is a unique individual possessing a cultural heritage that is diverse and interesting. He can feel free and comfortable to share a cultural commonality with European-Americans, African-Americans, Native Americans and Asian-Americans. **He refuses to be given an identity. He demands the right to choose his identity.** Every American should have this right and we MUST teach our young people that they must demand it as a means of moving beyond 'racial' and 'color' identities.

Though one may appear to be what is often called the 'black race' today, that very person may also have recent ancestors whose appearance may be very different than their own. They may have a European-American grandmother as the Rev. Dr. Martin Luther King and W.E.B. Dubois had. Or that person may have a European-American father as Frederick Douglass, and Booker T. Washington had. Or a European-American mother as the famous actress and model Halle Berry has. Or a great variety of cultural ancestries and heritages as Colin Powell, Tiger Woods have. Yours truly, the author's immediate ancestry includes Native American Cherokee, African-American, Irish-American and Dutch-American. Knowledge of my cultural heritages allow me to feel free share a kinship with Americans who don't look like me and for them likewise.

There are untold millions of Americans who claim to be 'white' or who are told that they are 'white' by various government agencies, who have, in fact, recent ancestors who are African-American, Latino-American, Asian-American, Native-American, or Pacific-Islander. Yet, for various reasons, they only go by the 'low informational' title of 'white'.

The title 'white' prevents us, as fellow Americans, from not only knowing more about that person, which also allows us to gather some idea of their behavior from their cultural norms, but also it prevents us from having the opportunity of having many interesting or revelatory discussions about that person's ancestry and how, perhaps, that person's culture may in fact be related to our own.

What 'low informational' titles, in essence, do for us is that it prevents us from recognizing and celebrating our commonality as Americans of diverse cultural heritages. They also prevent us from discovering that human identity is not fixed and immutable. Which brings to mind a very important point to remember from Jung Min Choi, who said, "As long as Americans understand 'race' to be a reflection of a fixed, immutable, and permanent trait of an individual or group, any significant changes to bring about equality are unlikely."3

1 – Dunn, Robert G., "Identity Crises" - 1998

2 – Helms, Janet, "Racial Identity in the School Environment" from "Multicultural Counseling in Schools" by Paul Pederson and John C. Carey

3 – Choi , Jung Min, "Racial Ontology, Inferiorization and Assimilation"

Chapter 16 How 'Race" Acts to Mask our Problems

"These [racial] 'chameleonic' concepts of are especially dangerous, for they hide their discriminatory or exclusionary significance behind more readily acceptable conceptual schemata."
– R. Wasserstrom in "Racist Culture" by David Theo Goldberg

"To understand 'race conflict,' we need to fundamentally understand 'conflict' and not 'race.'
                              – Ruth Benedict

"Human beings throughout the world are fundamentally alike . . . The basic differences between ethnic groups are cultural, and conventional norms serve as masks to cover the similarities."
– Kwan and Shibutani in "Race Consciousness" by Gary Peller in "Critical Race Theory" Crenshaw, Gotanda, Peller, Thomas.

A great majority of American institutions and Americans use 'race' to mask their very real social and personal problems that they just as well not admit to. It is important for those who teach the BOLD AMERICAN OUTLOOK understand that 'race' issues, 'race' conflicts and specifically 'race' statistics often camouflage more serious problems, usually problems that those who have power to correct don't desire to. Often talk or even action on these 'racial' issues – as 'affirmative-action' has shown – or 'racialzied' statistics rarely lead to any significant change or progress against the perpetuation of racism's legacy.

As alluded to in my chapters on 'hate crimes' and self-proclaimed 'racist,' certain Americans and some American institutions, just don't want to admit that <u>certain problems</u> – personally or institutionally – that seem non-resolvable, <u>are often due to various psychological or pathologies that seriously need appropriate medical attention</u>. Yet, if a serious problem is passed off as 'racial' simply because a person claims to be a 'racist' then the problem is ignored. In fact, the so-called 'racist' has just thrown a cloak on not only his eyes, but our eyes. Likewise, because a victim, of a crime or violent act, just happens to look different, has a different religion, sexual persuasion, etc. does not mean that the aggressor should be treated any different than for the crime committed. Murder is murder, assault is assault, rape is rape. It is only our historical record of allowing European-Americans who committed crimes and acts of violence to go free or receive little punishment for their actions that forged acceptance of 'hate crime' legislation.

But such laws do little to get to the heart of the matter. The question we should be asking more is this: Why are Americans so rude, disrespectful, unfair, criminal and violent toward our fellow Americans. Why?

One of the prime reasons we don't ask this question is because we think we already have the answer. We think it's racism. We think it's bigotry. We think it's ethnic bashing.   But we really can't get to the real reasons because they are buried below the camouflage and masks of racism's legacy.

I sincerely believe that once we rid ourselves of the perpetuated status of racism's legacy in American society, we can then and only then, begin to get to the real issues, the real problems, and finally discover what really makes us relate to one another the way we do – **the real conflict** – we have with one another.

This is an epiphany that perhaps only our young people will ever see, and it is our duty to help them achieve it. A BOLD AMERICAN OUTLOOK can help American young people throw off the baggage of racism's legacy. Peel of the layers of deceit, demeaning deception and degradation of our cultural selves.

When a person or even a society has a very real and serious problem but neglects to act under the guise that it's just too immense, too complex or unrecognizable, then that problem inevitably will fester and grow.   This is exactly what is happening with racism's legacy. Just because we don't consistently acknowledge it or talk about, does not mean that it has gone away.

Racism's legacy is still a major part of American society today not just because we perpetuate it daily in our American discourse, but also because we ignore the true realities and dynamics of that discourse as well. Racism's legacy will always be apart of the American ethos because of its long history. Yet, it should and can only be minor.

The tragedy now is that in many parts of the United States, racism is getting worse. We MUST acknowledge this, recognize what can be done – particularly by starting with our very young people – and begin the process of unloading the baggage that is the 'language of racism' and peeling of the mask that allow us to go about our daily functions without doing something about the obvious problems we share in our American societies, American schools and American homes.

Chapter 17 The Seductive Nature of 'Race' and 'Color'

"Our reliance on common sense racial notions subvert our ability to produce accurate theoretical or even descriptive accounts of our social and cultural circumstances."
- David Lionel Smith – "The House That Race Built"

The reality is that most Americans are so comfortable with the concept of 'races' and 'colored' people that we revel in it. We are obsessed with 'race' and 'color.' So much so that we are seduced by the relative emotive images of a 'mixed-race' couple or the symbolism of 'white' supremacy or 'Black Power.' Even such terms as the 'White House' or the 'Black Church' give us a sense of complacent comfort despite undertones of intended symbolism and oxymoronic absurdity.

The Dictionary of Bias-Free Usage states that, "Rev. Dr. Martin Luther King, Jr. pointed out that there are some 190 synonyms for 'blackness' of which at least half are offensive. Almost all the 134 synonyms for 'whiteness' are favorable." Robert B. Moore, in *Racism and Sexism* by Paula S. Rothenberg noted that, "The symbolism of white as positive and black as negative is pervasive in our culture. The good guys wear white hats and ride white horse, and everybody know what the bad guys wear and ride. Dictionary definitions of black refer in part to the evil, the devil, disaster, condemnation, dirt, sullenness, and darkness while definitions of white refer to innocence, purity, harmlessness, good fortune, and lightness. Avoiding these words that reinforce the negative connotations of black will not do away with racism, but it can lessen the everyday pain these expression cause readers."

The BOLD AMERICAN OUTLOOK is not intended to just avoid 'color' words because of their symbolic power. The notions of 'race' and 'color' have enough historical baggage that mere avoidance will not suffice. We must also understand the history and the concept behind the use of 'color' and most of all, why we continue to use them.

The present-day evidence of our seduction of 'race' and 'color' images include our belief in so-called 'white' supremacist and efforts to pass legislation that requires law enforcement agencies to note the 'race' of individuals who are pulled over for alleged traffic violations because of a current phenomenon known as DWB – 'Driving While Black.' The former requires a belief in the 'whiteness' of the supremacist, yet we rarely if ever here of 'black' supremacist. The latter requires not only that Americans of African phenotype must now check their 'color' before they turn that key, but also that law enforcement had better enhance their training on 'race' recognition. Or will all Americans be asked their 'race' along with their driver's license.

The hilarity and the absurdity of our 'color' consciousness make life painfully ironic and tragic. A reality that we can prevent our young people from reproducing and/or perpetuating through a BOLD AMERICAN OUTLOOK. Our seduction to 'race' and 'color' are further enhanced by the means by which government agencies using 'race' laced Census data distributes benefits and burdens to the people of this nation based on 'race.' (Appiah & Gutmann) 1996.

As most Americans understand it, that there are 'races' and 'colored' people is natural. As the conventional wisdom goes, we look different, therefore there ARE different 'races' and people ARE different colors, therefore there ARE 'colored' people. It just seems to make common sense. How can anyone deny the fact that certain groups of people are different?

Yet, most Americans do not recognize or realize the extent to which they have internalized the notions of a reality of 'races' and 'colors.' These notions originated from an old-world beliefs in major differences in the superiority and inferiority of the 'races' with the 'white race' being the most superior and the 'black race' being the most inferior.

The reality is that we are all more similar than alike and our differences are so minor as to be insignificant. Yet, the persistence of our 'racial' and 'colored' selves continues. Why?

The reasons are seductive. It's so easy for us to believe in something that seems or appears common sense than not, even when there is scientific proof to the contrary.   Jared Diamond noted in *Discover* magazines' "Race, What is It Good For?" issue that, "Science often violates simple common sense. Our eyes tell us that the Earth is flat, that the sun revolves around the Earth, and that we humans are not animals. But we ignore the evidence of our senses."

We have learned that our planet is indeed round and revolves around the sun, and that humans indeed are NOT 'races.' Yet, we'd just as well still believe that the world is flat! Americans – and any society that succumbs to the belief in 'races' – might as well be living in a time warp.

The BOLD AMERICAN OUTLOOK is an attempt to prevent America's young people from being trapped in the historical constraints, or even chains if you will, of that time warp. Years ago, in a published article, I wrote that, "It is unfortunate (and sadly ironic) that when we discuss the social phenomenon that is racism in America, we are held hostage by the very words and concepts that helped to legitimize this shameful social legacy." We must not allow our young people to be vulnerable to the seductive power of the 'language of racism.' This nation has been held hostage by its power for far too long. We must empower America's young people with the means to end racism's legacy.

Chapter 18 Who Perpetuates Racism' Legacy the Most?

"It is not 'race' but a PRACTICE of racial classification that bedevils [American] society."

– Yehudi O. Webster.

The BOLD AMERICAN OUTLOOK maintains that racism's legacy is perpetuated by the 'language of racism' – the various words and concepts of 'race,' ' color' and 'minority' status within the American discourse. Yet, who or what institutions are most responsible for this perpetuation?

Well, the great majority of adult Americans regardless of institution affiliation perpetuate racism's legacy through their use of the 'language of racism' either wittingly or unwittingly. Put simply, the great body of Americans who participate in the American discourse are most responsible for perpetuating the 'language of racism.' Yet there are some institutions that appear to be the most pervasive perpetuators or who do the most damage as far as sanctioning and continuing the use of 'race' 'color' and 'minority' terms.

While working as a journalist – when I first became suspicious of the manner and modes of how certain key words perpetuate racism's legacy – I was convinced that American media institutions were the greatest perpetuators of racism's legacy. No longer.

Educational Institutions

Now, after a decade of research and reflection, I am convinced that our schools – from pre-school to post-graduate colleges – do more to perpetuate the beliefs of 'race,' 'color' and 'minority' status – the 'language of racism – than any of our American institutions. Some may call it institutional racism, but I call it an institutional disgrace upon this nation. American schools still practice the classification of students into 'races.' Granted, most have begun to use cultural titles, but still they equate to 'races' and still the greatest emphasis always seem to gravitated to just two 'races' – 'white' or 'Anglo' and 'black.' America's schools have the greatest potential for instilling a sense of 'racial' identity because it is here that young people first learn that the various words of 'race' and 'color' are to be understood as valid concepts, that is, in regard to the traditional American discourse and beliefs.

There is hope though. As responsible educators and parents, concerned about the future health of relations in this nation, you have a viable option with the BOLD AMERICAN OUTLOOK. And, as educators or parents, you are in the best possible position to bring about change. American young people, particularly those in the early stages need to know there are alternatives to the 'language of racism' that will improve their chances for more meaningful relationships in the future. Also, by replacing 'racial' labels with cultural titles, young people will grow to understand that though there are some differences among Americans that, overall, what we share is our greatest asset – our American heritage.

America's colleges and graduate schools, despite their capacity for 'higher' learning, are notorious for perpetuating the 'language of racism.' Yet, they must get some recognition for at least having greater materials for research for understanding and ending racism's legacy – I know this all too well.

The Government

Second as the American institution that perpetuates racism's legacy the most is the American government institutions that ask Americans information about their 'race.' Boston Globe Columnist Jeff Jacoby noted in a 1997 article that, "The U.S. Census has always been obsessed with race. For decades it attempted to distinguish among degrees of blackness. Slaves had to be identified as 'black' [two African parents] or 'mulatto' [an African and European parent]. After 1890, 'mulattoes' were broken down further into 'quadroons' or 'octoroons.' These repulsive gradations were finally abandoned in 1920, when the government, harking back to the 'one-drop rule' declared it would deem anyone with any black ancestry at all as black."

(Interestingly, Albert Murray noted in *"The Omni-Americans"* that, "American culture, even in its most rigidly segregated precincts, is patently and irrevocably composite. It is, regardless of all the hysterical protestations of those who would have it otherwise, incontestably mulatto. Indeed, for all their traditional antagonisms and obvious differences, the so-called black and so-called white people of the United States resemble nobody else in the world so much as they resemble each other. And what is more, even their most extreme and violent polarities represent nothing so much as the natural history of pluralism in an open society.)

"A bigger mystery is why the government herds us into racial pens in the first place," continues Jacoby. "As scientist probe ever more deeply into the human genome, it becomes clear that race is just a social construct, not a biological one . . . So why should the government concern itself with racial categories at all?

"Not because such statistics don't have their uses, but because they are too likely to have their *mis* uses . . . Apply for a job, and you are asked your race. Bid on a public contract, and you are asked your race. Seek admission to college, try to get financial aid, request a home mortgage – and you are asked your race. From job promotions to congressional redistricting, we are increasingly viewed not as individuals but as members of racial groups. The government crunches numbers based on irrelevant criteria – skin color, eye shape – then uses those statistics to make decisions that affect us for life."

Jacoby also quotes Stephan and Abigail Thernstrom from their book "America in Black and White" (I did not really study this volume primarily because I found their continued use of 'black' and 'white' and 'race' derivative. And, scanning through it, I found it to be very history intensive and over-bound with statistics. In fact, a reviewer of the book, Martin Duberman, stated that it, "opens with six historical chapters about race relations in the 20th century; they contain no fresh scholarship and make for dull reading." I am compelled to offer this bit of cautious insight by them.) "It is tempting to halt the collection of all racial statistics by the Bureau of the Census, the Department of Justice and other government bodies. Those classifications pit members of one group against the other, poisoning the racial atmosphere."

Jacoby concludes that, "The more the government demands racial data and the more it makes outcomes depend on race, the more it pushes all of us to dwell on racial differences. The perverse reality is that racial statistics create racial divisions. It is not written in stone that governments must count their citizens by race. Canada hasn't had a racial question on its census since 1951."

Jacoby's article was one of the best written I've ever read concerning how we perpetuate racism's legacy unnecessarily and I encourage all who read this to request a copy of this Nov. 19, 1997 article from the Boston Globe. His article, along with Yehudi Webster's "The Racialization of America" represent the type of reasoned and critical attacks we all must begin to become accustomed to make ourselves if we want to teach a BOLD AMERICAN OUTLOOK to American young people.

The Media

Finally the American media is the last, but certainly not the least most prevalent institutional perpetuator of the 'language of racism' and racism's legacy. In fact, to many people the media, as I first believe, is THE most prevalent perpetuator of racism's legacy. There is some validity to that argument. I would position the media like this: The media has the greatest impact on our present-day associations and beliefs in the concepts of 'race' 'color' and 'minority' status. While the aforementioned institutions above have an effect that instills a sense of permanence to 'racial' 'color' and 'minority' classifications.

This nation's news media seems to be hopelessly obsessed with 'race' and 'color.' The reasons are all too clear why. Those in power in the media know that they have the power to evoke intense variations of emotions to a wide variety of Americans because of the historical memories and animosities inherent in racism's legacy. A cursory review of recent and past news media events will undoubtedly uncover more than an occasional story involving some kind of 'racial' incident, many sensationalized unmercilessly.

One aspect that showcases how America's TV and motion picture industries is obsessed in the manner by which they cast their movies or shows.

Invariably, the cast is just one culture group or predominately one culture group with a sprinkling of token non-predominate culture group cast members. TV talk shows, particularly the day-time-Jerry Springer-variety play 'racial' politics to its most optimum affect.

Radio also, is not immune from perpetuating 'racial' identities, particularly in America's urban areas. Here in Los Angeles, one of the most culturally diverse cities in the United States, notions of 'racialized' identities and politics are exploited and perpetuated by such radio 'personalities' as Larry Elder and Jon London on AM and FM stations respectively. Elder, a talk show host, claims he is 'black,' is shameless in his efforts to polarize and evoke conflict and hostility by playing to the emotions of his audience/callers whom he unabashedly recognizes as 'whites' and 'blacks' and 'races.'

The gist of the matter here is that Elder, decidedly middle-class and well educated consistently plays to the emotions of his 'white' audience who are nearly unanimous in their approval of his show. Likewise, a majority of the 'black' callers are in disagreement with Elder's views and he invariably is more hostile toward them than his 'white' callers, evidenced by the fact that African-American led groups have attempted to get him off the air and African-American community leaders refuse to talk on his show. Even worse, the show is essentially a comedy radio show that masquerades as a show dealing with serious issues, such as racism's legacy, which Elder frequently brings up as topics of discussion. His lack of respectful empathy for the African-American experience in this nation is particularly appalling to African-American male callers and what's worse is that he is a master at manipulating the manipulative nature of 'race.' The show is both a spectacle to marvel at and a disgrace in regards to its ability to worsen present-day and future human relations.

The overwhelming reason for the perpetuation of racism's legacy by these institutions are that those in positions of influence in the media have themselves been raised to believe that the old paradigms of 'race' and 'color' are indeed valid. Thus, they see no reason to alter what they believe is an accurate reflection of reality (or a reasonably appropriate reality, if they do understand the fallacies of 'race' and racism's legacy).

It would seem inappropriate, indeed to even suggest that images that the media projects are inaccurate, yet it is not entirely the images that are the most profound in perpetuating racism's legacy. Equally, if not more so in my opinion, is the message that the media projects, and that message invariably is that there are 'races' and 'colored' people and 'minority' people in the United States.

As you now know, this chapter does not shed any instructive light on how to show young people to avoid doing what these institutions are doing. Yet, I sincerely hope that it does shed some informative value in relation to how far our young people must go to undo what we are doing in regard to perpetuating racism's legacy.

Chapter 19 A Logical CONCLUSION

"If we, and I mean the relatively conscious so-called 'whites' and the relatively conscious so-called 'blacks,' who, like [new] lovers, insist on creating the consciousness of the other; if we do not falter in our duty, we may . . . end our 'racial' nightmare and achieve our country and change the history of the world."

– James Baldwin 1

What I've found most inspiring and most regrettable at the same time during my years of research for this book is how all of the admired writers, scholars and human biologist that I've cited herein have, in all due respect, failed to take their brilliant research and observations to the 'Logical Conclusion.'

Nearly all, with the notable exception of Mr. Montagu, seem to write or reveal their research, insights and ideas to the reader in a way that, if taken to heart by the reader, assumes that reader or readers can effectively begin to end racism's legacy then and there or at least a few years hence. The BOLD AMERICAN OUTLOOK does not hold that view. The BOLD AMERICAN OUTLOOK explicitly is a PROCESS that will take at least a generation to become effective. With your help, this process can begin immediately.

This is THE ONLY thing that makes the BOLD AMERICAN OUTLOOK unique: its intent is for American young people so that they can bring about effective solutions to racism's legacy. Solutions which can only be effective when they are infused without any references to the 'language of racism' or historical grievances – something that adults today and historically have demonstrated we cannot do. This is actually logical sense we adults have been socialized to actually believe in such things as 'race' and 'color' evidenced by its prevalent use.

The doomed realities of 'affirmative action' and 'hate crimes' demonstrate that infusing laws, policies and discourse with 'race' and other 'constructed identities' only lead to mask the real personal and social issue that needs to be pointedly addressed and also create unnecessary animosities and hostilities among Americans

I did not originate the concept that 'race' is not a human reality. I am not the first to claim that our use of 'color' terms (Davis, 1991) and 'minority' (Montagu, 1962) are non-existent and leads to errors in logic. I am not the first to state that the term 'Indian' is a fabricated, inaccurate and demeaning.

What the BOLD AMERICAN OUTLOOK promises to do that nothing else out there does is that it takes all these insights and harness them into a synergy of hope – something American young people honestly don't have in regards to racism. The BOLD AMERICAN OUTLOOK fosters taking all this information to its greatest possible logical conclusion – teaching it to America's young people.

The reality is, as even some the experts have shown, that adults who've already been socialized to think in terms of 'race' and 'color' still find it difficult, if not impossible, to think, write and speak in modes that do not further the classifications of humans as 'races' and 'colored' people.

Getting adults and educators to not do this is a primary goal of this book, which is why I have explicitly attempted to consistently place all references of 'race' and 'color' in single or double quotes – to bring attention to their so-called and non-reality nature.

Unfortunately, most of the experts did not do this, demonstrating that even their thinking and arguments are incased in thought processes of 'race' and 'color.' It is my sincere hope that we may be able to teach and show young people that this is something that they just MUST not do if they are ever to be able to rid themselves from 'racialized' thinking and thus clarity in their thinking. Montagu was the first that I've researched who made the connection between ridding oneself of 'racial' thinking as the first step toward clear thinking on our social problems and relationships.

Actually, Montagu makes an impassioned plea for teaching young people to focus on human relations, yet not in the same manner as the BOLD AMERICAN OUTLOOK, i.e. with a focus on eliminating just 'race.' The BOLD AMERICAN OUTLOOK is unique in its quest to rid our discourses of 'color' terms and 'minority' terms toward humans. Yet the BOLD AMERICAN OUTLOOK Principle are equally important toward bringing into focus the all-important '**point-of-view** that Charles Wilson so eloquently pinpointed as what was needed to combat racism in American education.

Of course it is just not the education realm that needs help with racism's legacy. This is why I intentionally did not just place the focus of this book on educators only. Parents are equally important, if not more important, for forging the beliefs and ideals of American young people. Yet, America's public school systems are the only American institutions where some form of city, state or national consistency is possible, therefore, this is my main focus and hope for American's young people.

I am convinced, as I sincerely hope you too are convinced, that the BOLD AMERICAN OUTLOOK has a positive and promising place in the future of our young people. I also sincerely believe that if the educator/ parent heeds to the examples detailed in this book and reads at least a few of the books in the included Bibliography, then that SYNERGY will energize you with the same hope that I have that a 'post-racism paradigm' can become a reality in the United States and in the hearts and minds of the future of this nation – our young people.

When effective solutions to racism's legacy are instituted they will be effective because a generation of American young people will have been raised and nurtured to understand the dynamics or racism's legacy. They will not be ignorant of the history of racism in the United States, they will have studied it and the BOLD AMERICAN OUTLOOK does not foster a view that the history of racism is not taught. The BOLD AMERICAN OUTLOOK basically intends to inform young people that racism is an historical construct that CAN be abolished in their lifetime if they use and apply the BOLD AMERICAN OUTLOOK principles and focus on solutions. This empowers them, for only they can bring about effective change. Without the inhibitions of the old 'language of racism' paradigms and with COURAGE, FAIRNESS, AND CULTURAL RESPECT they won't need Civil Rights laws or 'affirmative action' or 'hate crime' laws.

117

By embracing and celebrating other cultures, America's young people can use their courage to develop communities that embrace and encourage diversity because they know that it is in <u>their</u> child's best interest to grow and learn with young people of diverse cultural heritages. Also, today's young people will know from their learning of cultural respect, not to allow for the blurring or neglect of their culture and other cultures by consistently planning community-wide cultural events celebrating the various cultural heritages <u>and</u> traditional American culture within their community.

The overarching theme that young people must learn from a BOLD AMERICAN OUTLOOK is that a person's cultural heritage is the most important and significant thing about that person. The more we know about a fellow American's culture, the more we can cherish it, the more we can value it, and the more likely we can come together as a common people to end racism's legacy. Then and only then will America's young people – uninhibited by fears of other 'races' and with an informed knowledge of the contributions of Americans of diverse cultures – move forward in making the United States the most culturally wealthy and greatest nation the world has ever known.

1- James Baldwin – "The Fire Next Time" – 1963.

Appendix A – Just Who Are Americans

Americans are one or more of the heritages below and more:
(My apologies if I omitted your cultural heritage)

Americans of various **African heritages** – including: Belize-Americans, Brazilian-American, Cuban-Americans, Dominican-Americans, Haitian-Americans, Jamaican-Americans, Mexican-Americans, Native-Americans, Puerto Rican-Americans and of various African nations and groups i. e., Asante, Falani, Ibo, Yoruba, etc. and of various Caribbean, European and South American nations.

Americans of various **Arab heritages** – including: Iranian-Americans, Iraqi-Americans, and Saudi-Americans, Syrian-Americans, etc.

Americans of various **Asian heritages** – including: Burmese-Americans, Cambodian-Americans various Chinese-American groups, Hindu/India-Americans, Pakistani-American, Japanese-Americans, Korean-Americans, Laotian-Americans, Twainese-Americans, etc.

Americans of various **Australian heritages and New Zealand heritages**

Americans of various **Canadian heritages**

Americans of various **European-Americans heritages** – including: Albanian-American, Austrian-Americans, British/English-Americans, Czech-American, Dutch-Americans, Finnish-Americans, French-Americans, German-Americans, Greek-Americans, Hungarian-

American, Irish-Americans, Italian-Americans, Jewish-Americans, Norwegian-Americans, Polish-Americans, Russian-Americans, Swede-Americans, Swiss-Americans, Yugoslavian-Americans, etc.

Americans of various **Latino/Hispanic heritages** – including: Argentinean-Americans, Belize-American, Brazilian-Americans, Chilean-Americans, Colombian-Americans, Costa Rican-Americans, Cuban-Americans, Dominican-Americans, Ecuadorian-Americans, El Salvadorian-Americans, Haitian-Americans, Honduran-Americans, Mexican-Americans, Panamanian-Americans, Peruvian-Americans, Puerto Rican-Americans, Venezulan-Americans.

Americans of various **Jewish heritages** – world-wide

Native Americans of over **500 nation/heritages** including: Apache, Cherokee, Eskimo, Lakoda, Walla Walla etc. and **NOT Indian**

Americans of various **Pacific Islander heritages** including: Filipino-Americans, Guam-Americans, Hawaiian-Americans, Indonesian-Americans, Samoan-Americans, etc.

APPENDIX B

Award incentive ideas for all school levels. All nominees receive an I Have a BOLD AMERICAN OUTLOOK T-Shirt. Winner receives a plaque. The nominee certificates should be printed on pre-printed decorative certificate paper.

(Pre-SCHOOL)

MY STUDENT

---

has been nominated for

The BOLD AMERICAN
OUTLOOK

Award

By (teacher),

First Avenue School

(GRADE) SCHOOL

MY STUDENT

---

has been nominated for

The BOLD AMERICAN
OUTLOOK

Award

By (teacher),
_____

First Avenue School

(Middle School) SCHOOL

MY STUDENT

---

has been nominated for

The BOLD AMERICAN
OUTLOOK

Award

By (teacher),
_____

Madison Middle School

(High School)

MY STUDENT

---

has been nominated for

The BOLD AMERICAN
OUTLOOK

Award

By (teacher),
_____

Jefferson High School

Selected Bibliography

Adams, Michael Vannoy, "The Multicultural Imagination" 1996

Appiah, Kwame, A. "In My Father's House" – 1993.

Appiah, Kwame, A. "Europe Upside Down: Fallacies of the New Afrocentrism." From Times Literary Supplement (Feb. 12th, 1993).

Baldwin, James "The Fire Next Time" New York: Dial Press, 1963

Banton, Michael & Harwood, Jonathon, "The Race Concept" – 1975.

Benedict, Ruth, "Race, Science and Politics" – 1943.

Bennett, Lerone Jr., "Before the Mayflower" – 1988.

Callaghan, Karen A., 'Symbolic Violence and Race' in "Postmodernism and Race"

Choi, Jung Min, "Racist Ontology, Inferiorization and Assimilation" *from "Postmodernism and Race" – Eric Mark Kramer – 1997*

Comas, Juan, "Race Myths" – 1951.

Crenshaw, Kimberle "Critical Race Theory" - 1997

Davis, James – "Who is Black" – 1991.

Disch, Robert & Schwartz, Barry, "White Racism" – 1972.

Dunn, Robert G., "Identity Crises" – 1998.

Ferber, Abby L., "White Man Falling" – 1998.

Goldberg, David Theo, "Racist Culture" – 1993.

Gutmann, Amy & K. Anthony Appiah, "Color Consciousness" – 1996.

Helms, Janet, "Racial Identity in the School Environment" from "Multicultural Counseling in Schools" by Paul Pederson and John C. Carey

Haney-Lopez, Ian, "White by Law" – 1996.

Haizlip, Shirlee Taylor, "The Sweeter the Juice" – 1996.

Kivel, Paul, "Uprooting Racism" – 1996.

Kramer, Eric Mark, "Postmodernism and Race" – 1997.

Landrine, Hope & Elizabeth Klonoff, "African-American Acculturation" – 1996.

Locke, Don C., "Increasing Multicultural Understanding" – 1998.

Lubiano, Wahneema, "The House That Race Built" – 1998.

Molnar, Stephen, "Human Variation" – 1983.

Montagu, Ashley, "Man's Most Dangerous Myth – The Fallacy of Race" - 1964

Montagu, Ashley, "Race, Science and Humanity" – 1963.

Murray, Albert, "The Omni-Americans" – 1970.

Mydral, Gunnar, "An American Dilemma – 1944.

Omi, Michael & Winant, Howard, "Racial Formation in the United States" – 1986.

Pedersen, Paul, "Multicultural Counseling in Schools" – 1994.

Podair, Simon, in "White Racism" – Barry Schwartz and Robert Disch, 1972.

Rothstein, Stanley "Class, Culture and Race in American Schools"– 1995

Sue, et al., "Multicultural Counseling Competencies" – 1998.

Sowell, Thomas, "Race and Culture" – 1994.

Smith, David Lionel – "What is Black Culture" in "The House That Race Built" – 1997.

Tatum, Beverly, "Why Are All the Black Kids Sitting Together in the Cafeteria" – 1997.

Twomey, David P. – "Equal Employment Opportunity Law" - 1990.

Webster, Yehudi O. "Against the Multicultural Agenda" – 1997.

Webster, Yehudi O. "The Racialization of America" – 1992.

West, Cornel, "Race Matters" 1993.

Willie, Charles V. & Brown, B., & Kramer, B., "Racism and Mental Health" – 1973.

About the Author

I'm a Cultural Diversity Consultant based in California and I enjoy helping people to understand the true dynamics of "race" and "color" in the United States. I studied Journalism at California State University, Dominguez Hills, before beginning work as a reporter, editor and editorial consultant. While working as a journalist, I recognized how the media established practices that unreasonably furthered "racial" identities unnecessarily and I thus began a decade of research on racism's legacy in the United States.

This book is a result, not only of years of research of racism's legacy in America, but also of a lifetime of reflection on what my life experiences have been in a family whose heritage is obviously culturally diverse, but spoken only in terms of being either "black," "white" or "Indian." This book is the first in a series of books to address and correct these false identities for my family and all Americans.